KU-447-021

THREE ONE-ACT PLAYS

QUEEN MARGARET COLLEGE

100 065 872

THREE ONE-ACT PLAYS

Brian Clark *POST MORTEM*
Jim Hawkins *TOO HOT TO HANDLE*
Rosemary Mason *SUNBEAMS*

AMBER LANE PRESS

Post Mortem Copyright © Brian Clark, 1979
Too Hot to Handle Copyright © Jim Hawkins, 1979
Sunbeams Copyright © Rosemary Mason, 1979

All rights whatsoever in these three plays are strictly reserved
and application for professional performance should be made
to:
Judy Daish Associates,
Globe Theatre,
Shaftesbury Avenue,
London W1V 7AA.

Application for amateur performance should be made to:
Samuel French Ltd.,
26 Southampton Street,
London WC2E 7JE.

No performance may be given unless a licence has been
obtained.

First published in 1979 by
Amber Lane Productions Ltd.,
Amber Lane Farmhouse,
The Slack,
Ashover, Derbyshire S45 0EB.

Printed in Great Britain by
A. Wheaton & Co. Ltd., Exeter.

Typesetting and make-up by
Computerset (Phototypesetting) Ltd., Oxford.

ISBN 0 906399 08 4

CONDITIONS OF SALE
This book is sold subject to the condition that it
shall not, by way of trade or otherwise, be lent,
re-sold, hired out or otherwise circulated without
the publisher's prior consent in any form of binding
or cover other than that in which it is published
and without a similar condition including this condition
being imposed on the subsequent purchaser.

Brian Clark

POST MORTEM

Post Mortem was first produced at the Soho Poly, London, on 25th March, 1975, with Alison Fiske playing the role of Helen. A television version with Judy Parfitt as Helen was transmitted by BBC 2 on 7th July, 1975 and a radio version starring Fiona Walker was broadcast in May, 1976.

Characters

HELEN

Voices on the phone

TOPOLSKI
DOROTHY
IVENS
TOM
HERRIDGE
CORNFORTH
MR JOYCE
BRADLEY
VOICE FROM LEEDS
CHARLES
OPERATOR
PRESS MAN

SEIKERS
GIRL

Recorded voice

L.K. HALPIN

PRODUCTION NOTE

It is essential that the audience knows that L.K. Halpin is dead. In the stage production at the Soho Poly this was achieved by means of a projected slide showing Halpin lying dead across his bed, clutching his chest. In the picture we also saw the telephone and Ansaphone. The slide can be faded in each time the Ansaphone is used.

The voices at the other end of the phone were played by four actors sitting on high stools about the auditorium. Each was lit by a pencil spot while speaking.

SCENE ONE
L.K. Halpin's bedroom. Day.
The face of a Teasmade clock says 9 a.m.
L.K. Halpin, a man in his forties, is dead.
There is no sign of violence. His last move-
ment has been to grasp at his chest. A tele-
phone rings by the side of the bed.

SCENE TWO
L.K. Halpin's study.
The telephone here is connected to an ex-
pensive Ansaphone device. It clicks and we
hear the recording.

HALPIN: 'L.K. Halpin is not available at the moment.
If this is a personal call would you please
leave a message at the end of this recording
. . .'

[*A nearby Telex machine starts chat-*
tering.]

'. . . If it is a business call would you please
ring the office — 01 170 3000. Thank you.
Please leave your message — now — [*Beep*].'

SCENE THREE
L.K. Halpin's office.
The office is a huge room. Three-quarters of
it is pristine, polished and tidy: this part is
L.K. Halpin's. There is a vast empty desk
and a very large executive chair. The re-
maining quarter of the office is used by
HELEN ANSTY, *L.K. Halpin's Personal Assis-*
tant. Her desk shows signs of continuing
activity. The clock on the wall says a few
minutes after 10 a.m.
HELEN ANSTY *enters and immediately begins*
to take off her coat, registering slight
surprise that L.K. is not already at work.
HELEN *is thirty-four, dressed elegantly but*

unostentatiously. On her desk she places a pile of letters and the Financial Times. *She crosses to the Telex machine and reads the message that was transmitted in Scene Two. The telephone on her desk rings. She crosses to answer it.*

HELEN: L.K. Halpin.

OPERATOR: I have a call from New York.

HELEN: Yes.

> [*She smiles slightly and glances towards the Telex machine.*]

TOPOLSKI: Hello?

HELEN: L.K. Halpin. Can I help you?

TOPOLSKI: Is Mr Halpin there?

HELEN: Not yet, I'm afraid. This is Helen Ansty, his personal assistant. Can I give him a message?

TOPOLSKI: This is Furnival Securities here. I'm Jacob Topolski.

HELEN: Ah, yes. We've received your Telex.

TOPOLSKI: Tell him ... it's fantastic ... When L.A. closed, Smeitcher had jumped 23 points. Christ knows what it'll do in New York this morning. It must be worth half a million already.

HELEN: You did buy at 2.59, didn't you?

TOPOLSKI: Of course ...

HELEN: Then perhaps when trading begins you'd sell. Please.

TOPOLSKI: ... Sell? But the price could go on rising ...

HELEN: Mr Halpin isn't a gambler, Mr Topolski, and I do have his instructions ...

TOPOLSKI: Well, he's sure a lucky man.

HELEN: Mr Halpin's always quoting Mark Twain: 'The harder I work, the luckier I am.'

> [*While the conversation continues,* HELEN *is looking through the morning letters.*]

TOPOLSKI: [*chuckling*] Well, I don't know how he could
have worked at this. The news broke right
out of the blue. Some Japanese company is
going to completely rejig, using Smeitcher
products — Nippon Metals.

HELEN: I'll telex confirmation to sell the stock.

TOPOLSKI: If that's what you want . . .

HELEN: Yes.

TOPOLSKI: I'm not saying we couldn't use the commis-
sion. Our exchange is just like yours. More
like a morgue than a market.

HELEN: Good morning, Mr Topolski.
[*She replaces the telephone then
presses a button on her intercom
unit.*]
Dorothy?

DOROTHY: Morning, Miss Ansty. Sorry I'm a bit late.

HELEN: Send off a Telex to Furnival Securities, New
York, instructing them to sell the Smeitcher
stock immediately, please.

DOROTHY: Yes, Miss Ansty. How is your mother?

HELEN: Just the same. I'll probably be going up there
this weekend. Hurry with the Telex.

DOROTHY: Yes, Miss Ansty.
[*From one letter* HELEN *takes a small
tape cassette. She registers slight surprise then quickly fits it into her
recorder. She switches it on.*]

HALPIN: Morning, Helen. This is L.K. You won't be
seeing me today.
[HELEN *looks towards the empty
chair behind the desk.*]
Dr Hasting's just given me a real roasting.
Said if I didn't ease up there'd be no point
booking a summer holiday. So I'm going to
do what I'm told for a change and have a lie
in. Course, I'll probably be awake hours
waiting for the bloody Teasmade to work. So

you're the boss for today. That means just keeping your finger in the hole in the dyke and hoping like hell the bloody thing doesn't breach somewhere else. If that Smeitcher deal clicks you'll have to get rid of our holdings in T.K.L. Trust. Break the connection with Nippon Metals. There was another great fuss in the F.T. today about insider dealing. As though the only ones allowed to make money ought to be people with no stake in anything. We'll pull Sandy out of Nippon, we don't want to be caught with interests in either. So do it quietly, love. No fuss. One last thing. That bloody Sheikh's money — five million should arrive soon. If it comes today get it into Hatton Fields Property as soon as you can. God knows when we'll be able to develop that site — even if we got the corner piece — but we've got to show *some* activity on it to keep up confidence. If the price of Hatton Fields Securities drops any further the bloody merchant banks will be squealing for their money. So the loan from our mysterious Sheikh of Araby will keep them happy for a bit. But every silver lining has a cloud. The wily bugger will only invest on a week's recall of the money. It seems he doesn't have much confidence in Sterling. He's only letting us have it because inflation eats it away marginally less slowly than the rats in his tent. So have fun, love, and if anything exciting happens, let me know. I'll be here — bored stiff.

> [*The tape ends.* HELEN *switches off the machine. She flicks the intercom switch.*]

HELEN: Dorothy?

DOROTHY: Yes, Miss Ansty?

HELEN: It seems that Mr Halpin won't be in today . . .

DOROTHY: Really?

HELEN: . . . Could you get me Ivens and Crayshaw, please? I want Mr Ivens.

DOROTHY: OK.

> [HELEN *switches off the intercom. She walks to the main desk and opens Mr Halpin's engagement book. Her telephone rings.*]

HELEN: Yes?

DOROTHY: Mr Ivens for you.

HELEN: Hello.

IVENS: Hello! You're bright and early this morning . . .

HELEN: Things are happening early this morning.

IVENS: L.K. steaming around no doubt. Buying the earth and selling it back to God at a modest 23% profit . . .

HELEN: As a matter of fact, he's having a day off.

IVENS: I don't believe it.

HELEN: It's true . . . he's having a rest today.

IVENS: My God! Well, don't let the news leak out. The market's only just coping anyway. But the fact that L.K. is having a rest would probably take 50 points off the F.T. Index.

HELEN: I think I can just about manage for one day.

IVENS: Of course you can, my dear, of course . . . how tactless of me. Why, with his capital and your looks you could get a 24% profit from God.

HELEN: I don't know that I'd sell to him — I'd have to see what better offers I could get.

IVENS: Well, you know, there's always one offer you've got.

HELEN: And how's Mrs Ivens this morning?

IVENS: Blooming, he said ambiguously . . . Well, if you're turning down exciting offers this morning . . . what boring thing can I do for you?

HELEN: Start to sell our holdings in T.K.L. Trust. Slowly and unostentatiously.

IVENS: Why . . . ? There's no point. I know liquidity is difficult at the moment but surely . . . Hang on a minute . . . didn't I see some Los Angeles prices this morning?

HELEN: Now, now, steady on . . . a stockbroker must make four from two and two. It's us that makes five.

IVENS: All right, my dear . . . I'll start easing out . . . like a ghost in plimsolls.

HELEN: So long as nobody gets frightened!

IVENS: It shall be done with the discretion of a bishop in a brothel!

HELEN: I hope you don't mix your clients' accounts as much as your metaphors. Bye!

> [*She rings off then clicks down the intercom.*]

Dorothy . . . L.K. had an appointment with Mr Halstein at three o'clock. Ring up and cancel, will you? Say we'll ring tomorrow. Say pressure of work . . . don't tell him he's away today.

DOROTHY: OK.

SCENE FOUR
L.K. Halpin's office. Later.
HELEN *is busy doing paper work. Her direct line rings.*

HELEN: L.K. Halpin.

TOM: You crept away this morning. I didn't even know you were gone.

HELEN: You looked so peaceful, I didn't want to disturb you. Started work yet?

TOM: Well . . . sort of . . . let's say I'm researching.

HELEN: Oh? Into what?

TOM: The basic daily research of the freelance journalist is the newspapers . . .

HELEN: I see! You're drinking coffee and reading the papers . . .

TOM: You could put it like that. And what are you doing? Apart from making millions for that tycoon of yours.

HELEN: He's not mine, darling.

TOM: I need proof of that.

HELEN: More?

TOM: The proof I really need is that you marry me and have babies so that you can't creep out of my bed and go back to your tycoon.

HELEN: Careful. I might accept your proposal one of these days.

TOM: . . . If you don't soon, I might stop making them.

HELEN: Not so serious, so early in the morning . . .

TOM: Why not? I love you in the mornings as well . . .

HELEN: I know . . . and I love you.

TOM: Great. So why don't you see that you're working in a cancer ward. It's terminal, love. You can only keep the patient alive with drugs that will kill him.

HELEN: L.K. isn't that ill. Just a heart murmur.

TOM: I'm not talking about L.K. but the whole city. Now why don't you move in with me and then into a maternity ward. That's where life begins!

HELEN: Tom . . . !

TOM: All right. All right. I promise not to propose to you again until lunchtime.

HELEN: Ah, I was going to ring you about that actually . . .

TOM: Oh no! Your tycoon has suddenly discovered that lunch in the Savoy would be desolate without you.

HELEN: No . . . he's not here. I'm holding the fort and I'd rather stay . . . I'll send out for a sandwich or something.

TOM: Surely you can spare a half an hour or so . . . I've got to be in the City . . .

[*The intercom buzzes.*]

HELEN: Hang on, Tom . . . [*She clicks the intercom switch.*] Yes . . . ?

DOROTHY: There's a call from Mr Herridge.

HELEN: I won't be a minute . . . ask him to wait a moment. [*into the phone*] Tom, I've got to ring off . . . there's an important call.

TOM: Please see me for lunch — just for half an hour.

HELEN: All right, Tom . . . call for me then . . . only half an hour, mind!

TOM: OK. See you, bye.

HELEN: Bye. [*She replaces one phone and picks up another.*] Hello, Helen Ansty here.

HERRIDGE: Hello, is L.K. there?

HELEN: 'Fraid not. He's away today.

HERRIDGE: Damn! Can I get in touch with him?

HELEN: Is it important?

HERRIDGE: Very . . . I've got Kemble in the other office. He's ready to sell the shop on the corner of Hatton Fields site.

HELEN: Can't it wait till tomorrow?

HERRIDGE: I've been working on him for weeks. Got his creditors to squeeze him . . . everything. L.K. knows all about it. That corner piece is the key to the whole site. Without it the rest isn't worth a can of beans.

HELEN: What's it worth now?

HERRIDGE: Well, *with* the corner site, just about a can of beans.

HELEN: So what's the hurry?

HERRIDGE: We had to keep quiet about collecting the properties on Hatton Fields so the prices wouldn't rise. Well, now, with the last piece, we could make a splash. It's all a question of confidence. Everybody will *want* to think we can make a go of it. So the price of Hatton

AMBER LANE PLAYS
Series Editor: Judith Scott

Contents

Post Mortem Copyright © Brian Clark, 1979
Too Hot to Handle Copyright © Jim Hawkins, 1979
Sunbeams Copyright © Rosemary Mason, 1979

All rights whatsoever in these three plays are strictly reserved
and application for professional performance should be made
to:
Judy Daish Associates,
Globe Theatre,
Shaftesbury Avenue,
London W1V 7AA.

Application for amateur performance should be made to:
Samuel French Ltd.,
26 Southampton Street,
London WC2E 7JE.

No performance may be given unless a licence has been
obtained.

First published in 1979 by
Amber Lane Productions Ltd.,
Amber Lane Farmhouse,
The Slack,
Ashover, Derbyshire S45 0EB.

Printed in Great Britain by
A. Wheaton & Co. Ltd., Exeter.

Typesetting and make-up by
Computerset (Phototypesetting) Ltd., Oxford.

ISBN 0 906399 08 4

CONDITIONS OF SALE
This book is sold subject to the condition that it
shall not, by way of trade or otherwise, be lent,
re-sold, hired out or otherwise circulated without
the publisher's prior consent in any form of binding
or cover other than that in which it is published
and without a similar condition including this condition
being imposed on the subsequent purchaser.

THREE ONE-ACT PLAYS

Brian Clark *POST MORTEM*
Jim Hawkins *TOO HOT TO HANDLE*
Rosemary Mason *SUNBEAMS*

AMBER LANE PRESS

QUEEN MARGARET COLLEGE LIBRARY

Fields Securities will stay up, for the time being at least.

HELEN: But good money after bad ...

HERRIDGE: We're not going to go bust for one and a half grand. We're in for millions. We've no choice.

HELEN: Hang on ...

[*She picks up the other phone and dials rapidly. We hear the Ansaphone recorded message.*]

HALPIN: 'L.K. Halpin is not available at the moment ...'

HELEN: [*to* HERRIDGE] I can't get him for the moment. It'll have to be tomorrow.

HERRIDGE: Listen, we've squeezed him so hard through his creditors, he'll sell to anybody. Christ, he's already selling it to us so cheap, it would almost pay a spec builder to buy it to put a bungalow on it. For God's sake ...

HELEN: So it's got to be now ...

[HELEN *looks at L.K.'s empty chair. The intercom buzzes.*]

Hang on ... yes?

HERRIDGE: Oh Christ!

HELEN: Who is it?

DOROTHY: From Kent Whittaker's merchant bank. A Mr Joyce.

HELEN: All right ... tell him I won't be a moment ...

[*She switches off the intercom, touches L.K.'s cassette on the desk, then speaks into the phone.*]

OK, Mr Herridge ... buy it.

HERRIDGE: I've got to have a cheque right away ... to press into his hot little hand ...

HELEN: I'll have it sent round. How much?

HERRIDGE: Ten per cent should do ... say fifteen thousand.

HELEN: Right ... you'll have it in a few minutes.

HERRIDGE: Great.

[HELEN *rings off and picks up the other phone.*]

HELEN: Helen Ansty.

MR JOYCE: Hello, Miss Ansty, is L.K. about?

HELEN: 'Fraid not. Having a day off.

MR JOYCE: That's unusual, isn't it . . . ? Nothing wrong I hope.

HELEN: No, just everything's quiet, that's all.

MR JOYCE: Unfortunately not that quiet. I did want a word with him.

HELEN: Can I give him a message?

MR JOYCE: It's this Hatton Fields business.

HELEN: Oh yes.

MR JOYCE: As you know, the loan from us was secured by Blacks Secondary Bank Stock. Well, they stopped trading months ago and we still don't know what the stock is worth — if anything. That didn't matter really as long as the titles to the Hatton Fields properties were a good investment, but . . . well . . . you've no doubt seen the prices . . .

[HELEN *punches up the price on the Reuters video screen.*]

And I think the other directors would be happier if L.K. could arrange some other security for the loan.

[*The intercom buzzes.*]

HELEN: Excuse me. [*She clicks the intercom.*] Yes?

DOROTHY: It's Mr Cornforth, Miss Ansty.

HELEN: One moment. [*into the phone*] Sorry about that, Mr Joyce, I've an incoming call from our solicitors.

MR JOYCE: Do get L.K. to give me a ring.

HELEN: Yes, of course.

MR JOYCE: He'll have to think of something. I mean, Hatton Fields looks just like a desert now. It's hard to think what to do with it in the present circumstances . . . one of the other directors was saying that the only hope for it was to strike oil or gold on it ... those are about the only things worth having these days, eh?

HELEN: Yes ... I'll get L.K. to ring very soon.

MR JOYCE: Yes, I should be pleased ... bye.

[HELEN *rings off and picks up the other phone.*]

HELEN: Helen Ansty. That you, Hugh?

CORNFORTH: That's right.

HELEN: Sorry to keep you waiting. One of those days.

CORNFORTH: And how is our high-powered lady?

HELEN: Firing on all four cylinders.

CORNFORTH: So what skulduggery is old L.K. up to now?

HELEN: None at all. Far from it. Everything's so serene he's taken the day off.

CORNFORTH: Has he now? That's a turn up for the book ...

HELEN: Yes ... Now what can we do for you this morning?

CORNFORTH: Well actually, there's a cheque for five million sitting staring at me from my desk, with all its six eyes.

HELEN: That's nice for you.

CORNFORTH: Well, yes ... but unfortunately it's not mine — it's L.K.'s. From the oil sheikh chappie he was having the odd word with.

[*The intercom buzzes.*]

HELEN: Hang on a minute, Hugh. [*She clicks the intercom.*] Yes?

DOROTHY: It's Leeds Infirmary, they say it's urgent.

HELEN: I'll be one moment. [*into the phone*] Sorry Hugh ... I'll have to hurry. An urgent call. That five million, it's for the Hatton Fields Account. It'll cheer it up a bit.

CORNFORTH: Righty-o. Will do.

HELEN: Bye Hugh. Sorry to rush. [*She slams down the phone and picks up the other one.*] Helen Ansty.

VOICE: This is the Leeds Infirmary here.

HELEN: Yes.

VOICE: Not very good news, I'm afraid ... Are you the daughter of Celia Ansty?

HELEN: Yes ... what's wrong?

VOICE: I'm afraid your mother is rather ill. She was admitted an hour ago ... she's suffered a stroke ...

HELEN: A stroke! But I was speaking to her on the phone yesterday ... I'm sorry — that's silly ... How ill is she?

VOICE: Very seriously, I'm afraid. The doctor feels that you should try to see her as soon as possible.

HELEN: I see ... Is she conscious?

VOICE: Intermittently. She's rather confused ... but she did ask for you.

HELEN: I'll get up there as soon as possible. Thank you very much. If you want me soon, ring 246 1117. It'll put you straight through to me.

VOICE: Yes. Goodbye.

[HELEN *rings off. She sits back a moment to absorb the news. She clicks on the intercom.*]

HELEN: Dorothy, find out the times of the next three trains to Leeds, will you please?

DOROTHY: OK.

[HELEN *clicks off. Still shocked, she walks to a wall safe, opens it and takes out a cheque book. She goes back to her desk and writes out a cheque. She picks up the phone and dials rapidly.*]

HALPIN: 'L.K. Halpin is not available at the moment. If this is a personal call ...'

[*With irritation,* HELEN *clicks on the intercom.*]

HELEN: Dorothy, come and collect a cheque and have it sent round right away to Mr Herridge.

DOROTHY:	I'm still trying to get Train Enquiries — you know what they're like . . .
HELEN:	Leave it a moment and get this cheque off.
HALPIN:	'. . . Thank you. Please leave your message — now — [*Beep*].'

SCENE FIVE
L.K. Halpin's study.
We hear HELEN*'s voice on the Ansaphone.*

HELEN: 'L.K. No chance of your being bored. Everything's happening today, First, can you ring Joyce, please? Kent Whittaker's are anxious about the security of the Hatton Fields loan on the Blacks bank stock. It's down to 20p and likely to go bust. Joyce does want alternative security. I'm sorry, but you'll have to ring him up, please. Second, Kemble has agreed to sell the Hatton Fields corner site. As you know, Herridge had pressed him very hard and wanted a cheque for fifteen thousand pounds. To make sure Kemble couldn't change his mind. I'll have a cheque sent round. Finally, I'm afraid I have to go up to Leeds straight away. My mother has had a stroke. I'm sorry about this but I'll ring you from Leeds and I'll be back in the office in the morning. I hope you're having a restful day . . . By the way, Ivens is beginning to sell the T.K.L. Trust holdings.'

SCENE SIX
L.K. Halpin's office.
HELEN *is replacing the phone. She picks up the cheque book and walks over to the wall safe. She is thinking hard. She picks up a phone and dials.*

TOM: Hello, Tom Evans speaking.

HELEN: Tom, Helen here.

TOM: No, I'm not going to cancel our lunch date.

HELEN: Have to, sorry . . .

TOM: You tell that bloody tycoon . . .

HELEN: It's my mother . . . in Leeds. She's had a stroke. I've got to go up straight away . . .

TOM: Darling, I'm sorry . . . really . . . it's serious, is it?

HELEN: Sounds . . . sort of final.

TOM: Oh . . . look . . . I'll come up with you.

HELEN: Would you? But your article . . .

TOM: Sod that. I'll do it some time. What train are you catching?

HELEN: Don't know yet. We haven't been able to get enquiries . . .

TOM: I've got a rail guide here. I'll look it up . . . hang on.

[HELEN *clicks the intercom.*]

HELEN: Dorothy . . . forget the Leeds trains. A friend's looking it up for me.

DOROTHY: OK. I've sent off the cheque . . .

HELEN: Good . . .

TOM: Here we are . . . Leeds . . . it's from King's Cross. 11.25.

HELEN: It's a bit soon . . . I might miss that one.

TOM: The next is 13.10 . . . that's a long time. Hang on, there's one from St Pancras at 12.05.

HELEN: That'll do.

TOM: See you at the barrier then. I'll get the tickets. It arrives 15.40.

HELEN: Let's hope it's in time.

TOM: Try not to worry, darling.

HELEN: No . . . and thank you, Tom.

TOM: It's nothing . . . see you.

[HELEN *rings off. She takes a deep breath and starts to tidy her desk, throwing away the notes she's made. The intercom buzzes.*]

DOROTHY: Mr Ivens for you.

[HELEN *picks up the phone.*]

HELEN: Hello, Mr Ivens.

IVENS: L.K. still not available?

HELEN: No, I'm afraid you'll have to put up with me.

IVENS: No problem . . . but I've just picked up a rumour on the floor. Thought L.K. ought to know.

HELEN: Yes?

IVENS: A journalist has been making enquiries about T.K.L. and Nippon Metals . . .

HELEN: Oh? Who?

IVENS: Clive someone or other . . . Bradley . . . Clive Bradley.

HELEN: Hang on . . . [*She clicks the intercom.*] Dorothy, get 239 6048 for me, please.

DOROTHY: OK.

[HELEN *clicks off.*]

HELEN: [*into the phone*] What did he want to know?

IVENS: Just nosing around, really — as far as I could gather. I couldn't press too hard in case the jobber I was talking to thought there was something in it.

HELEN: What should we do, then?

IVENS: Nothing, I suppose . . . just go even more slowly.

[*The other phone rings.*]

HELEN: Hang on.

[*She picks up the other phone and holds the 'Ivens' phone against her shoulder.*]

TOM: Hello . . . any news?

HELEN: No . . . it's not about that. Something's cropped up. Do you know of a journalist called Clive Bradley?

TOM: Yes . . . what about him?

HELEN: What's he like?

TOM: Bloody good. Freelance . . . left-wing . . . has a fantastic nose for dirt. Is he after L.K.?

HELEN: No, no! Nothing like that. So, he's your

	honest-to-goodness, hand on the heart, genuine ... muck-raker, is he?
TOM:	That's right! Incorruptible, so don't try. It'll make it worse.
HELEN:	I've told you ... it's nothing to do with L.K.
TOM:	Hm!
HELEN:	Anyway, thanks.
TOM:	See you 12.05.
HELEN:	Yes ... bye. [*She puts down the phone. to* IVENS.] Hello?
IVENS:	Hello.
HELEN:	Bradley is a left-wing muck-raker. He's evidently very good — and incorruptible.
IVENS:	My God ... you must have a fantastic filing system there. So, what do we do?
HELEN:	Nothing.

[*The intercom buzzes.*]

DOROTHY:	Mr Herridge on the line for you.
HELEN:	Put him through. [*to* IVENS] I'll let L.K. know and we'll keep in touch. Let us know if you hear anything more. Bye. [*She rings off and picks up the other phone.*] Helen Ansty.
HERRIDGE:	L.K. still not about?
HELEN:	No.
HERRIDGE:	You'll have to get hold of him. Now.
HELEN:	Why?
HERRIDGE:	Downing has just been arrested.
HELEN:	Who on earth is he?
HERRIDGE:	The Planning Officer. He was about to sew up the whole Hatton Fields development.
HELEN:	Does his arrest involve us?
HERRIDGE:	Not yet. It's to do with a roads contract or something. But it could come out — and soon. In any case, the Hatton Fields development will be gone over with a fine tooth comb now.
HELEN:	Hold the line a moment, please. [*She clicks the intercom.*] Dorothy, ring L.K. at home.

[*into the phone*] So Hatton Fields is a dead duck now.

HERRIDGE: For the foreseeable future. For us anyway . . . and it could be worse. If Downing mentions certain transactions . . .

[*The intercom buzzes.*]

DOROTHY: I'm getting the Ansaphone.

HELEN: Then send somebody around to tell him he's got to answer the bloody phone himself . . . Taxi! And ring all the numbers we have. Find him! [*into the phone*] So what shall we do?

HERRIDGE: Sit tight, I suppose.

HELEN: What about the cheque for fifteen thousand? Could we stop it?

HERRIDGE: We could but that would just draw attention to ourselves. That's only fifteen thousand, we're in for over five million. On the other hand, that deal is security for two or three others. It's like a house of cards. We've got to get L.K. He'll have to rearrange everything, so if Hatton Fields folds up, it doesn't bring the rest down.

HELEN: Hang on . . . [*She clicks the intercom.*] Dorothy, get the solicitor, Dakworth and Harlow's, please — Mr Cornforth.

DOROTHY: I'm trying to find Mr Halpin.

HELEN: Then get somebody else to get Cornforth. There's enough of you, aren't there?

DOROTHY: Sorry, Miss Ansty.

[HELEN *clicks off the intercom.*]

HELEN: [*into the phone*] Now let's get this clear. It looks as if the Hatton Fields project is about to fold and we'll be left with an investment of five million that we can't develop.

HERRIDGE: You will be. Don't forget I'm just an agent in this.

HELEN: Come off it. Stop trying to separate yourself.

It's too late. Your business is too tied up with ours to survive if we don't.

HERRIDGE: I know that. L.K. didn't hire us to play pat-a-cake with Kemble, but I just want to make it clear that we didn't have anything to do with inducing Downing to get us planning permission.

[*The intercom buzzes.*]

DOROTHY: [*haughtily*] Mr Cornforth, Miss Ansty.

HELEN: All right ... one moment ... any news of L.K.?

DOROTHY: No, we're still trying!

[HELEN *clicks off the intercom.*]

HELEN: [*into the phone*] Hold on, Mr Herridge, I'll be with you in one moment. [*She lays the receiver down on the desk and picks up the other phone.*] Hugh?

CORNFORTH: Twice in under an hour, what a pleas—

HELEN: Have you paid that five million into the Hatton Fields account yet?

CORNFORTH: ... No, I don't think so ... I'll see ...

HELEN: Find out and if you haven't, don't, repeat *don't* ... I'll be with you in a moment. [*She lays the receiver down and picks up the other phone.*] Mr Herridge?

HERRIDGE: Yes?

HELEN: Now look, are you saying that L.K. personally bribed Downing?

HERRIDGE: No, of course I'm not. I don't know anything about it. You should know about that.

HELEN: Well, I don't. That's not the way L.K. does business. All I'm concerned about is to untie the five million.

HERRIDGE: Of course.

HELEN: You'll stay in your office, will you?

HERRIDGE: Yes.

HELEN: I'll be in touch. [*She rings off and picks up the other phone.*] Hugh?

CORNFORTH: Yes?

HELEN: Have you sent that cheque round to the bank?

CORNFORTH: It's back on my desk, looking at me with its . . .

HELEN: Thank God for that. Look, the Planning Officer dealing with Hatton Fields has been arrested — some road contract or other.

CORNFORTH: Naughty man. But nothing to do with L.K. . . . ?

HELEN: Of course not . . .

CORNFORTH: No, of course not . . . but . . . but in this wicked world people will start to put two and two together.

HELEN: Especially on the floor of the Exchange.

CORNFORTH: And Hatton Fields Securities, already doing a death-defying act, will suddenly get a shove — downwards.

HELEN: That could happen, couldn't it?

CORNFORTH: One doesn't have to be a financial expert to see that — or even a financial journalist.

HELEN: The first thing to do is to put that five million somewhere else. If Hatton Fields crashes, there's no point in losing that . . .

CORNFORTH: Absolutely not. But where, dear lady, shall I put it?

HELEN: Oh, I don't know. Somewhere safe.

CORNFORTH: I could put it under my mattress but even a day's interest on five million takes some paying.

HELEN: . . . Buy gold shares.

CORNFORTH: Gold shares!

HELEN: Yes . . . they're safe at the moment. And do it soon.

CORNFORTH: You'll get L.K. to send the instruction round.

HELEN: *I'll* send it round. If you've any worries, look in your safe, you'll find I have power of attorney.

CORNFORTH: Reprimand accepted.

HELEN: Oh Hugh, I'm sorry I'm so bitchy. L.K.'s away and everything's happening.

CORNFORTH: They'd still happen if he was there.

HELEN: But he'd be taking the decisions. Get in touch with Ivens straight away, will you, and get that money placed.

[*The intercom buzzes.*]

Excuse me a minute. [*She clicks the intercom and holds her hand over the phone.*] Yes?

DOROTHY: There's a Mr Bradley on the phone to speak to Mr Halpin.

HELEN: Bradley ... ? Is that Clive Bradley ... ?

DOROTHY: That's right.

HELEN: Tell him he's not available.

[*She clicks the intercom off, then thinks a moment. She reaches forward quickly and clicks on the intercom again.*]

Dorothy, ask him to hang on. Tell him I'll speak to him in a couple of minutes. [*She clicks off the intercom and picks up the phone.*] Sorry about that, Hugh ... Look, we've got to do something to stop the price of Hatton Fields Securities going too far down. Otherwise the merchant bankers will get really nasty.

CORNFORTH: Easier said than done.

HELEN: I've an idea. I'm going to start a rumour that big oil money is beginning to flow in to back the company.

CORNFORTH: Dangerous game.

HELEN: I know. I'm also going to get Ivens to buy some Hatton Fields shares. Fairly ostentatiously. Not too many. Just enough to back the oil money rumour.

CORNFORTH: But sooner or later rumours come home to roost and you either have to put up or shut up.

HELEN: Sooner or later! Christ, Hugh! The game we're playing in the City is a day-to-day business. If you're still there at four o'clock you pass 'Go' and collect two hundred pounds. If things don't turn up soon we're finished anyway. The thing is to stay in as long as possible. And hope.

CORNFORTH: All right. If that's what you want but I ought to warn ...

HELEN: Yes, I know. Sorry to cut you off but I've got a lot to do. Look, Hugh, ring Ivens now, will you? Buy those gold shares and tell him to use up to one hundred thousand pounds he's realised on T.K.L. shares to buy Hatton Fields Securities shares ... got that?

CORNFORTH: Gold ... one hundred thousand T.K.L. .... Hatton. Right ... but I do advise you to get in touch with L.K. before you do anything.

HELEN: Of course. I'll be in touch soon. Bye. [*She rings off and clicks the intercom.*] Is Mr Bradley still on the phone?

DOROTHY: Yes.

HELEN: Look, I need ten minutes to think and do one or two things ... either get his number or ask him to ring back. Be nice ... I do want to speak to him.

DOROTHY: All right.

> [HELEN *clicks off the intercom then picks up the phone and quickly dials. We hear L.K. Halpin's recorded message again.* HELEN *is exasperated. She lays the phone down to wait for the end of the record. She clicks the intercom on.*]

HELEN: Could you get the accountants, Levinson and Sons. It's Mr Jacobs I want.

DOROTHY: Right.

> [*By this time the recorded voice has finished.*]

SCENE SEVEN
L.K. Halpin's study.
We hear HELEN's *voice.*

HELEN: 'L.K. . . . you've got to ring in. The whole
lot's on the skids. We've got to convince Kent
Whittaker's that we can cover the losses on
our shares in Blacks Banks. The shit's really
hit the fan in the City. Joyce wants new cover
now. On top of that, Downing's been nicked.
Please, L.K., please ring in! I'm going to do
something but you can still stop it if you ring
in soon. I'm going to leak that really big
petro-dollars are flowing into Hatton Fields
and I've instructed Ivens to buy enough of
our own shares to back up the rumour. For
God's sake, L.K., ring in. Now.'

SCENE EIGHT
L.K. Halpin's office.
HELEN *is replacing the phone. The inter-*
com buzzes. HELEN *clicks it on.*

DOROTHY: Mr Jacobs has gone to lunch.
HELEN: Lunch! My God! What's the time?
[*She looks up at the clock. It is just
after 12 noon. The phone rings. She
picks it up.*]
Hello?
TOM: Helen! Is that you?
HELEN: Yes.
TOM: Don't you know the time? I'm at St Pancras.
HELEN: I've just seen it . . . oh Tom!
TOM: What are you doing? You can't get the train
now . . .
HELEN: It's chaos here . . . I just couldn't . . . I mean
I'm the only one who knows how every-
thing fits together . . . I mean . . . L.K.
TOM: Oh bugger L.K.! Your mother!

HELEN: Don't Tom . . . I'll catch the next train . . . I'll see you . . .

TOM: No, you won't.

HELEN: . . . Tom.

TOM: Not anywhere! Not ever.

HELEN: Tom!

> [*But he has rung off.* HELEN *is upset. The intercom buzzes.*]

Yes?

DOROTHY: Marion has just rung in. She's been ringing L.K.'s doorbell for ten minutes. But she can't make him hear. She wants to know what to do next.

HELEN: Tell her to come back. He must have gone out somewhere.

DOROTHY: Righto.

HELEN: And you'd better send out for a sandwich or something . . . we're going to be busy for a couple of hours.

DOROTHY: Oh, Miss Ansty . . . I was hoping . . .

HELEN: I don't care what you were hoping . . . and find out the next three trains for Leeds.

DOROTHY: I thought you said . . .

HELEN: I know what I said . . . don't argue, Dorothy, just do as I say. Now get me Clive Bradley, then Seikers and Partners, the PR firm, then the accountants — no, get them first — then Mr Ivens, then Mr Herridge. Have you got all that?

DOROTHY: Yes.

HELEN: When I give you two buzzes, get the next person . . . all right?

DOROTHY: Yes.

> [HELEN *clicks off the intercom. She stands up and moves over to the Telex.*]

HELEN: [*reading*] '. . . increasing concern at the crisis in the affairs of Hatton Fields Securities. It is reliably reported that . . .'

> [*The phone rings. She picks it up.
> She adopts a 'feminine' voice and
> 'chatters' in the call.*]

And what can I do for you, Mr Bradley?

BRADLEY: I was hoping to have a word with Mr Halpin.

HELEN: I'm afraid that just isn't possible. He's resting . . .

BRADLEY: Is he ill?

HELEN: Oh no. Nothing like that . . . I do assure you. Really . . . just a day off . . . nothing more.

BRADLEY: Methinks the lady doth protest too much.

HELEN: [*smiling to herself*] I'm sure I don't know what you mean . . . Can I help you?

BRADLEY: I don't know . . . I was just checking out a hunch really . . . just a lucky fluke, noticing that T.K.L. Trust had an interest in Nippon Metals.

HELEN: And how does that affect us?

BRADLEY: I'm not sure. I was hoping you'd tell me.

HELEN: We do have some T.K.L. stock but really, I think, just to spread the portfolio. It keeps a steady price and we could realise it quickly, that's all . . . sort of liquidity with interest.

BRADLEY: Nothing more?

HELEN: I'm sure not. L.K. used to deal in stocks quite a lot but lately . . . well, our main interest is property, you know.

BRADLEY: How to get rid of it, you mean.

HELEN: Come on, Mr Bradley, your red slip is showing. In fact only today we finished tying up a very important parcel of land.

BRADLEY: Sounds interesting. You must be the only ones still buying the stuff.

HELEN: Well, we are. You'll be aware we have been collecting land at Hatton Fields for a while. Today it all came together . . . I'm speaking off the record, of course . . . !

BRADLEY: But you'll never be able to finance building.

The City is flat on its back.

HELEN: You sound pleased about it.

BRADLEY: I'm not weeping much. It's only ever been a glorified Ladbrokes. Now it's a tatty corner betting shop. But just as irrelevant.

HELEN: There's more than one opinion about that. But even if it were true, the City's not the only place to get money.

BRADLEY: But no one in Europe, or America if it comes to that, could be daft enough to invest in British property at the minute.

HELEN: How insular you Socialists are becoming these days. There is money left in the world, you know.

BRADLEY: Yes . . . in the Middle East . . . wait a minute . . . are the Sheikhs . . . ?

[HELEN *presses the intercom twice.*]

HELEN: Look, it's been a lovely chat but I must go . . . there's an important call coming in . . .

BRADLEY: There's just one more . . .

HELEN: I'm frightfully sorry . . . I must go . . . Look, why don't you get in touch with our PR firm? Seikers and Partners. They'll tell you all you want to know.

[*The lights fade.*]

SCENE NINE
L.K. Halpin's office. Later.

HELEN: Yes, that's right, Mr Seikers. Bradley . . . I want him to get the impression that we are backed by big oil money . . . nothing dramatic, you know. Deny it, of course, but leave him some space between the lines.

SEIKERS: What's going on, then?

HELEN: Can't stop to explain. Just float that news . . . gently mind. See if you can avoid the leak being traced.

[*The lights fade.*]

SCENE TEN
L.K. Halpin's office. Later.

HELEN: But surely things aren't as bad as that?

CHARLES: They're not brilliant, are they? A question of confidence, really ...

HELEN: You're our accountants, surely you can assure them.

CHARLES: I've done everything I can.

HELEN: Well, I shouldn't tell you really. It's very secret but we are getting massive backing from certain quarters shall we say not too far east of Cairo.

CHARLES: Oil money!

HELEN: Steady, I didn't say that. But if things get really tight, you could just hint that we're not really worried.
[*The lights fade.*]

SCENE ELEVEN
L.K. Halpin's office. Later.

HELEN: No, I'm sorry, he's away for the day.

GIRL: Mr Joyce would like a word with him. He says it's urgent.

HELEN: I'll let you know the minute he gets in.
[*The lights fade.*]

SCENE TWELVE
L.K. Halpin's office. Later.

HELEN: Good, Mr Ivens ... it's going well, then.

IVENS: Depends what you want. As soon as it was known I was after property shares, I was knee-deep in jobbers.

HELEN: Don't let it go to your head. You've only got a hundred thousand pounds.

IVENS: But they want more information. The floor's alive with rumours. About oil money,

sheikhs, God knows what. I'll have to tell
them something.

HELEN: Tell them nothing.
[*The lights fade.*]

SCENE THIRTEEN
L.K. Halpin's office. Later.

HELEN: We don't usually give statements to the City
Press. Seikers and Partners handle our PR.

MAN: But can you confirm that Hatton Fields
Securities are being backed by petro-dollars?

HELEN: No.

MAN: But do you deny it?

HELEN: I have no statement to make.
[*The intercom buzzes.*]
Goodbye . . . Yes?

DOROTHY: Mr Joyce. He absolutely demands to speak to
you.

HELEN: All right, put him on. [*She picks up the
phone.*] Helen Ansty here.

MR JOYCE: I want to speak to L.K.

HELEN: I'm afraid he isn't available.

MR JOYCE: I must insist.

HELEN: It's no good Mr Joyce. He just isn't here.

MR JOYCE: . . . Then you tell me. What's the truth
behind all these rumours?

HELEN: I feel that L.K. himself should tell you.

MR JOYCE: And so do I, Miss Ansty, so do I.

HELEN: But surely, Mr Joyce, Hatton Fields has gone
up 10 points. You're not so worried about
the collateral.

MR JOYCE: They've gone up 10 points in four hours.
They could fall 20 in four minutes. We're
bankers, Miss Ansty, not bookmakers. If the
rumours are soundly based, fine. Things
would look much healthier. But if it's just a
delaying tactic, my fellow directors would
take a very serious view of that.

HELEN: I'll get him to ring as soon as possible.

MR JOYCE: Please. I must insist before eleven tomorrow. We have a board meeting then and I must report on this matter or I'm afraid serious action must ensue.

> [HELEN *rings off and stands up, exhausted. She looks up at the clock. It is 3.40. She presses the intercom.*]

HELEN: That's it, Dorothy. I've done all I can. I'll get the 17.05 train.

> [*She walks over to the Telex. The phone rings. She walks back and picks it up.*]

Helen Ansty.

IVENS: Ivens here. The most fantastic thing.

HELEN: What?

IVENS: Have you seen the Telexes?

HELEN: Not for an hour or two.

IVENS: There's the strongest possible rumour that the U.S. Government has agreed to raise the price of gold. The market's gone mad. Prices have jumped 40% and still rising.

HELEN: You bought . . .

IVENS: Yes, of course . . . three hours ago.

HELEN: Should we sell?

IVENS: Up to you but the last Telex said the U.S. Government was ordering an enquiry into Treasury security so it seems real.

HELEN: OK, hold on then. If anything looks dodgy, don't wait to ring, sell.

IVENS: Right . . . L.K. is fantastic. How did he know?

HELEN: Ah, that's his secret . . . Look, Mr Ivens, as soon as you have something on paper, send over 40% of the gold shares to Kent Whittaker's, will you? That'll still leave our five million in our hands, won't it?

IVENS: Oh yes.

HELEN: Good . . . do that, then. Bye.

> [*She rings off, then leans back and laughs. She buzzes the intercom.*]

Get Kent Whittaker's — Mr Joyce.

> [*She begins to tidy her desk. The intercom buzzes.*]

DOROTHY: Mr Joyce.

HELEN: Put him through. [*She picks up the phone.*] Mr Joyce?

MR JOYCE: Yes.

HELEN: Helen Ansty here. I've some news . . .

> [*The phone rings.*]

Excuse me a minute.

> [*She picks up the phone.*]

VOICE: Miss Ansty?

HELEN: Yes?

VOICE: This is the Leeds Infirmary here. Bad news, I'm afraid, I have to tell you that your mother died at 3.35 . . . hello?

HELEN: Yes . . . I'm here . . . did she say anything . . . ?

VOICE: She sent you her love.

HELEN: Thank you.

> [*She puts the phone down mechanically.*]

MR JOYCE: Hello? Hello?

> [HELEN *picks up the other phone.*]

HELEN: Sorry, Mr Joyce. I've rung to tell you that our stockbrokers will be delivering two million in gold shares as added security for our Hatton Fields loan.

MR JOYCE: Two million . . . well I'll be . . . What's that wily old devil been up to all day? The City running round in circles about L.K.'s property shares while he cleans up in golds.

HELEN: I take it that will satisfy you for the time being.

MR JOYCE: Of course, my dear. Mind you, I never thought L.K. would land himself in real trouble . . . he's too sharp for that . . . I'll bet he's listening on an extension. L.K., you'll buy me a double whisky when I see you at the Club for all the sweating I've done for you today.

HELEN: I must go . . .

MR JOYCE: Of course, my dear. I'll look forward to receiving the certificates.

HELEN: Goodbye.

[*She rings off then starts to dial again.*]

SCENE FOURTEEN
L.K. Halpin's study. Evening.
We hear the Ansaphone recorded message.

HALPIN: 'L.K. Halpin is not available at the moment. If this is a personal call would you please leave a message at the end of this recording . . .'

SCENE FIFTEEN
L.K. Halpin's bedroom.

HALPIN: '. . . If it is a business call would you please ring the office — 01 170 3000. Thank you. Please leave your message — now — [*Beep.*] [*We hear* HELEN's *voice.*]

HELEN: L.K. you live to fight another day. Today you made at least two million pounds. Perhaps you should take the day off more often.

[*There is a click.* HELEN *has rung off.*]

THE END

Jim Hawkins

TOO HOT TO HANDLE

Too Hot to Handle was first shown on BBC 2 on 2nd December, 1974. It was directed by Pam Brighton, produced by Barry Hanson and designed by Stanley Morris, with the following cast:

SUZANNE MITCHELL	Jane Wood
PETER MITCHELL	William Hoyland
VAL	Diana Rayworth

Characters

SUZANNE MITCHELL
PETER MITCHELL
VAL

THE SET

The set should suggest a modern suburban bungalow, decorated and furnished in the lower middle class fashion. It is neat and tidy — almost obsessively so — but not unusually affluent. There are three areas: kitchen, lounge and bedroom — in that order across the stage. The kitchen area has a small worktable, on which is ready-prepared salad and coffee. The lounge area has a settee, sideboard, dining table and television (facing upstage). The bedroom has a double bed, wardrobe and a large mirror (also facing upstage) on a dressing table.

Ideally the rear wall of the lounge has a false wall in front, which may be flown out. Or a cloth is set down the face of it, which may be pulled over between the scenes, revealing the specially dressed wall behind. The table cloth must also be swiftly removable.

SCENE ONE

Afternoon.

SUZANNE MITCHELL is the creator of this small domestic paradise and her life is plainly dedicated to its upkeep. She is in her middle to late thirties, an attractive but not glamorous woman who prefers dresses to trouser suits and wears slippers with fluffy bunny tails on the toes. She is the even-tempered but not very exciting product of Sunday School and Grammar School, not dim but not intellectual. She tends to see life as a dull but necessary routine imposition of order on disorder. She is what every nice mum would like her nice son to marry.

We find SUZANNE hand-sewing the cuffs on a new dress she has been making. It is a nice enough dress but not likely to win any prizes for daring. The table in the dining area has a sewing machine on it and various bits and pieces of sewing gear. The coffee table in the lounge area has two new cups of steaming instant coffee and a few biscuits on a plate. She is maybe listening to Woman's Hour on the radio.

The front door bell chimes. SUZANNE puts her sewing down, turns off the radio and goes through to answer the door. It's VAL. She is about the same age as SUZANNE but slightly more racy in style. Unlike SUZANNE, she probably smokes.

SUZANNE: Hello Val . . . It's really sweet of you to pop round so fast.

VAL: I wasn't doing anything.

SUZANNE: I've made some coffee . . . go on in.

> [VAL *goes through. The telephone rings as* SUZANNE *is passing it, and she answers.*]

SUZANNE: 97511 ... Oh, hello darling ... That's very sweet of you ... How about some chops ...? I've got carrots ...

> [*In the lounge* VAL *looks round, picks up the dress, examines it, pulls a face, puts it down and sugars some coffee.*]

Will you be back at the usual time ...? Yes ... Val's here ... I've just about finished my dress ... Course I'm a clever girl ... See you later, then ... bye, love ... bye.

> [*She blows a kiss into the phone and puts it down. She goes into the lounge.*]

That was Peter. He was just going to the shops so he rang in case there was anything I wanted.

VAL: That's nice.

SUZANNE: He likes to pop out of the bank in the afternoon now he's under-manager.

VAL: Why?

SUZANNE: Just to prove he can, I suppose.

VAL: I must say, I like being on my own, but it would be nice to have a man ringing me up.

SUZANNE: What about Harry?

VAL: It's not that sort of relationship.

SUZANNE: He seems nice enough.

VAL: That's about all. I need a bit more than 'nice'.

SUZANNE: Oh ... I nearly had you married off again.

VAL: No fear.

SUZANNE: Go on with you.

VAL: Not Harry.

SUZANNE: I thought you really liked him.

VAL: I think it was just the excitement of having a new man after a year off. Once I'd got over that I realised he was very boring ... Let's have a look at your dress.

SUZANNE: It's very simple, but I took a fancy to the material.

VAL: Oh . . . That's nice.

SUZANNE: It's a remnant. I got it in the market for 20p.

VAL: I'll have to go and see what they've got. I could do with some new clothes.

SUZANNE: It's a very easy pattern.

VAL: How long did it take you?

SUZANNE: Couple of hours.

VAL: It'd take me a couple of weeks.

SUZANNE: If you really want to make something I'll give you a hand any time.

VAL: Would you really?

SUZANNE: Course I will.

VAL: I'd like to make a trouser suit.

SUZANNE: It's a bit more difficult than a dress. I think I've got a pattern upstairs. I made one last year for the bank's staff outing. I'll show you . . . have you finished your coffee?

VAL: There we are.

SUZANNE: It'll be easier in the bedroom. There's a full-length mirror in there.

> [SUZANNE *gathers the dress and pins and leads the way.*]

They've had a lot of fun and games in the bank recently. The computer keeps breaking down.

VAL: They always do. Did you see that thing in the paper the other day about the computer that sent somebody an electricity bill for five million pounds?

SUZANNE: Isn't it ridiculous? I'd rather have my affairs looked after by people any day.

VAL: People break down too.

SUZANNE: At least they know what makes sense.

> [*They progress into the bedroom.* SUZANNE *draws the curtains and puts the light on.*]

Pins.

> [*She strips her dress off. She wears a long slip under it — nothing too*

> *sexy. She puts on the unfinished dress.*]

You must get a bit lonely sometimes.

VAL: Now and then. I'm better off without him.

SUZANNE: I don't know what I'd do without Peter ... ouch ... ! Left a pin in there ...

VAL: Got it.

SUZANNE: Ooh ... ! I suppose I'm just lucky.

VAL: You are.

SUZANNE: I mean, he's not Errol Flynn ... but we just ... get on together.

VAL: It's a good fit.

SUZANNE: I'm quite pleased with it.

> [*She examines herself in the mirror.*]

VAL: Where do you want the hem?

SUZANNE: About there.

> [*She fixes a point only just above the knee: a modest length.*]

VAL: D'you think so ... ? I'd put it a bit higher.

SUZANNE: You've got better legs than I have.

VAL: Don't be ridiculous.

SUZANNE: You have.

> [VAL *pulls* SUZANNE'S *dress up to show her legs.*]

VAL: You've got nice legs.

SUZANNE: They're too fat. [— *or whatever nasty thing the actress can bear to say about her legs!*]

VAL: Rubbish.

> [VAL *scrambles to her feet, pulls her dress up as well, and they stand side by side like a couple of chorus girls, comparing their legs in the mirror.*]

I think we've both got nice legs.

SUZANNE: Well ... just a little bit higher then.

> [VAL *pins up the hem.*]

VAL: Another one there ... ? That looks straight.

SUZANNE: I never feel ... quite right showing my legs.

> [VAL *mutters something through a mouthful of pins.*]

D'you think I'm stuffy?

VAL: A bit ... reticent maybe ... not that it's any of my business ... They're your legs ... There you are.

[SUZANNE *inspects herself, turning in front of the mirror.*]

SUZANNE: Can you just check once more that it's straight?

VAL: That's fine.

SUZANNE: Val ... you're an angel.

VAL: If I'm an angel, I'm a very reluctant one.

[SUZANNE *heads for the door.*]

Did you remember about that trouser suit pattern?

SUZANNE: Oh yes ... Let me think ... It might be in here.

[*She checks a drawer in the dressing table.*]

No. [*checking another drawer*] No ... Wait a minute, I think I put some patterns in a box in Peter's wardrobe.

[*She goes to* PETER's *wardrobe and opens it. It is full of sober clothes, and there is a high shelf with various boxes on it. She stretches up and grabs a box.*]

VAL: Do you want a chair?

SUZANNE: It's OK ... Can you take it from me?

VAL: Right.

[SUZANNE *heaves the box. It slides off the shelf and as it does so a stack of magazines and pictures underneath it cascades all over* VAL.]

Ow!

SUZANNE: Sorry.

[*She turns and as they ease the box down they both see that the books and pictures are pornographic pin-ups of girls showing their all. Maybe*

                        [*SUZANNE drops the box of patterns. She is really shocked. VAL is faintly amused, but adapts her reaction to SUZANNE's.*]

VAL: Well, well.

                        [*They both pick up a magazine and flick through.*]

So that's what I look like on a lonely Friday night.

SUZANNE: Errrhh!

                        [*SUZANNE drops the magazines in disgust.*]

VAL: 'Thirty Danish Darlings — Open Crutch Special.'

SUZANNE: Put it down!

                        [*VAL looks at her, sees her face, stops smiling and puts the magazine down.*]

I don't know what to say.

VAL: Didn't you know about . . . ?

SUZANNE: Of course I didn't . . . Why on earth does he want this filth?

VAL: You'd better ask Peter that.

SUZANNE: I will.

VAL: Or maybe you'd better put them back on the shelf and forget all about it.

SUZANNE: What would you do?

VAL: I'm not you.

SUZANNE: It's revolting . . . I had no idea.

VAL: Shall I pick them up for you?

                        [*VAL starts to look at them again but SUZANNE takes them from her and gathers them into a pile.*]

SUZANNE: I'll get that pattern for you. [*She fishes in the box.*] You won't . . . say anything, will you?

VAL: Of course not.

                        [*SUZANNE hands over the pattern.*]

SUZANNE: Thanks, love . . . I'm sorry.

VAL: What for?

SUZANNE: I'm sorry you saw ... that.

VAL: Doesn't bother me. Well, I'd better be off ...
It's a smashing dress. Bye-bye, love.

> SUZANNE *starts to collect the photos together. She forces herself to look at them and begins to study them, obviously trying to overcome her initial shock. She picks one up — a full-length, provocative, crutch-forward pose — and takes it over to the bed. She lays it face up on the cover. The obvious comparison brings her near to tears. She takes off her dress and in her underslip looks at herself in the mirror. She attempts to look at her own sexuality in a way that is new to her: defiant.*
> *Fade to blackout to the sound of a snatch of an ironic song such as* Darling, you can count on me *or* Everybody's doing it. *Under the blackout the rear wall of the lounge is flown, rotated or uncovered. It is covered with porno pin-ups. The lamp is rotated and has a girl on it. The table cloth is removed. The table has rude ladies spread as a cloth. The lights remain down in this area until later.*

SCENE TWO

Evening.
It's dark outside. SUZANNE *is in the kitchen, just completing a salad. She stirs some tea in the pot. She is smiling and maybe singing along.* PETER *comes in. He is the same age as* SUZANNE. *A neat man, with a quiet, serious*

voice and manner. He looks kind but a little dull. He has a coat and a briefcase. SUZANNE *is very friendly.*

PETER: Hello darling.
SUZANNE: Hello.
PETER: What's that?
SUZANNE: I decided to save the chops for tomorrow, if that's all right with you.
PETER: You're the boss . . .
           [*He kisses her affectionately on the nose.*]
SUZANNE: Had a good day?
PETER: Nothing special.
SUZANNE: Computer behaving itself?
PETER: Not a glitch in sight.
SUZANNE: Not a what?
PETER: Glitch . . . That's what you call it when a computer does something it's not supposed to.
           [*He starts to take his coat off.*]
SUZANNE: Sounds like a nasty skin disease . . . Can you toss that salad for me . . . I'll hang your coat up.
PETER: Oh . . . all right.
SUZANNE: I never get it all over the lettuce.
PETER: It's all a question of wrist action.
           [*She slips through into the darkened lounge with his coat.* PETER *tosses the salad with gusto.* SUZANNE *returns.*]
           You're looking very pretty this evening, if I may say so.
SUZANNE: Thank you.
PETER: What are you smiling at?
SUZANNE: Compliments.
PETER: Did you get your dress finished?
SUZANNE: Yes. Pour the tea.
PETER: I'll have a look at it after tea.
SUZANNE: I've invited Val round for a few drinks.

PETER: Fine.

SUZANNE: I think she's a bit lonely.

PETER: Cast your bread upon the waters.

SUZANNE: What's bread got to do with it?

PETER: It's the Bible, love ... You ought to know that ... 'Cast your bread upon the waters and it shall return unto you seven-fold.'

SUZANNE: It's not a bad rate of interest ... but then who wants soggy bread?

PETER: What I mean is ... she led Michael a right old dance, and now he's gone, and she's lonely.

SUZANNE: I suppose that's what Michael told you?

PETER: More or less.

SUZANNE: And he never cast any bread himself, as you put it?

PETER: Well ... it takes two.

SUZANNE: You've been reading 'A Banker's Guide to Psychology' again, haven't you?

PETER: No ... I just don't think she'd ever be happy with one man.

SUZANNE: Why have you got such a thing about poor Val?

PETER: I have not got a thing about her.

SUZANNE: But you don't like her?

PETER: I think she's a bit ... obvious.

SUZANNE: You wouldn't give her an overdraft?

PETER: On the contrary ... I never give overdrafts to people I like ... Infallible rule of banking.

SUZANNE: Bring the salad.

PETER: Right ... I'm quite hungry.

SUZANNE: Good.

> [*They go through to the dining area. Using dressmaking pins, SUZANNE has pinned pages of the porno magazines all over the walls, and the table cloth is a vast spread of buttocks and breasts, with plates neatly laid on it. PETER sweeps in to the table with the*

QUEEN MARGARET COLLEGE LIBRARY

> *salad bowl and doesn't register until he is there. He spills the salad on the table.*]

Now look what you've done ... She's got sauce vinaigrette all up her armpit!

> [PETER *takes off on a quick guided tour of the room but doesn't progress far before he stops. Then he sits down.*]

Your tea's getting cold.

PETER: Is this supposed to be funny?

SUZANNE: Come and eat your tea before Val gets here.

PETER: Take it down!

SUZANNE: Oh come on Peter ... I was looking for something in the bedroom and I found all these nice reproductions, so I thought, what's the point in hiding it away in a musty old cupboard when we could sit and look at it ... It's quite Christmassy, isn't it ... ? Don't be such an old fuddy-duddy ... What's the matter ... ? Don't you like it?

PETER: You had no right to do that.

SUZANNE: If you've got nice things you want people to see them, don't you ... ? Which one's your favourite ... ? I bet it's the blonde over the telly.

PETER: All right ... you've made your point.

SUZANNE: Some of the words are very nice too. [*She moves along the wall, reading out captions.*] '"When I was thirteen I used to make love to my pillow," says Tania ...' Oh look ... there's Tania's pillow ... That's a nice pillow case ... [*She walks nearer, still reading.*] 'Wendy was taking a bath when we came round. "Don't stop," we said, passing her the soap ...' D'you know, whenever I stick my legs up like that in the bath, I slip down and get my hair wet.

> [*The front door bell chimes.*]

I expect that's Val.

> [*She goes out of the hall door.* PETER *dashes round the room, ripping down pictures.* SUZANNE *is back before he's finished.*]

It was only the paper boy . . . Peter . . . ? Why are you taking the pictures down . . . ? Leave them up for Val to see . . . [*harder*] What's the matter . . . ? Don't you like them?

PETER: Stop playing stupid games.

SUZANNE: If you don't like them, why did you buy them?

> [*She goes back to her 'nice' voice and reads some more captions.*]

SUZANNE: 'The first thing Pat does when she gets back from the office is strip all her clothes off and rub herself with scented oil. She starts by smoothing it into her arms, but she soon works her way down over her throat to her breasts . . .'

PETER: All right!

> [*He goes to tear down the one she is reading. But she stops him, and they struggle a bit.*]

SUZANNE: Leave it alone!

> [*He turns away from her and takes down all the other pictures. He has a job getting the picture off the TV screen.*]

Why don't you ask Wendy for some soapy water?

PETER: You would have to make a scene, wouldn't you?

SUZANNE: I thought of posting them to the bank.

PETER: Couldn't you just talk about it?

SUZANNE: No.

PETER: Look . . . I'm sorry.

SUZANNE: You're not.

PETER: I said I'm sorry!

SUZANNE: You're sick.

PETER: I am not sick.

SUZANNE: I suppose you stand at the bottom of stairs and look up women's skirts as well.

PETER: No.

SUZANNE: When I was at school there were always little boys who wanted me to go behind the toilets and *show* them things.

PETER: And did you?

SUZANNE: Of course not.

PETER: As I thought.

SUZANNE: I imagine most of them are grown up by now. You'd expect them to by the time they're thirty-seven!

PETER: It's got nothing to do with you.

SUZANNE: I see. The fact that you obviously get some kind of satisfaction from seeing Wendy in her bath and Pat rubbing herself with scented oil has got nothing whatsoever to do with me. Neither has Amanda's Ice Cream Party or the particularly pleasing Thirty Danish Darlings!

> [PETER *concludes his fingernail job on the TV screen and now goes to the table and begins scraping the salad back into the bowl and then removes the pictures from under the plates.*]

Did you think you could keep them there for ever without me finding them?

> [PETER *screws up the pictures, fetches a newspaper and begins to wrap them up.*]

PETER: I thought you'd ignore it.

SUZANNE: The way you ignore me?

PETER: That's not true.

SUZANNE: It's the way I feel.

PETER: Well, you feel wrong.

> [*He carries the bundle out through the kitchen. Sound of a dustbin lid.*

He comes back into the room.]
Look . . . I've thrown them away. Let's just
forget it.

SUZANNE: Is that what you want?

PETER: Yes.

SUZANNE: All right darling.
[*He comes over.*]

PETER: It was just one of those silly things, you
know . . . ? I'm sorry.
[*He tries to kiss her but she rejects
him.*]

SUZANNE: Don't bring those eyeballs near me. I know
where they've been.
[*He turns away.*]
I'm quite hungry.
[*She goes to the table and starts to eat.
After a pause he joins her at the table.
He becomes 'normal' again.*]

PETER: What time's Val coming round?

SUZANNE: She should be here any minute.

PETER: Have we got some sherry in?

SUZANNE: Yes.

PETER: Good.

SUZANNE: We've always got sherry in.

PETER: We have been known to run out.

SUZANNE: Then I buy some more. And I do it all without the aid of a computer . . . [*pause*] Why
did you start ripping the pictures down
when you thought Val was coming?

PETER: It's nothing to do with her.

SUZANNE: Is that all?

PETER: I told you . . . It's just between you and me.

SUZANNE: Don't you mean you and you?

PETER: You know what I mean.

SUZANNE: Don't you want Val to think that you're a
dirty old man?

PETER: I thought we'd already established the fact
that I don't *like* Val.

SUZANNE: What's liking got to do with it? Do you have

to *like* the girls in the pictures . . . ? She's got
very big breasts . . . huge in fact . . . There she
is, three doors away . . . all on her own, dying
for a big hairy bank under-manager to rush
in and . . . peep up her frock.

> [*A pause.* PETER *attempts to change
> the subject by another enforced
> normality.*]

PETER: It's a nice salad.

SUZANNE: Let's hope it lasts.

PETER: Why?

SUZANNE: As from tomorrow I'm going to serve you
pictures of food.

> [PETER *pulls a face but carries on
> eating.*]

You really *didn't* want Val to see those
pictures, did you?

PETER: No.

SUZANNE: That's all right then . . . we'll forget it . . . I
shouldn't give her much sherry, though.

PETER: Why not?

SUZANNE: It might be embarrassing if she wants a pee.

> [PETER *takes a few seconds to realise,
> then throws his fork down and dashes
> out. He comes back, sad and be-
> wildered, screwing up more pic-
> tures.* SUZANNE *watches him.*]

'Peter was sitting on the stairs when we
arrived. "Don't stop," we said, passing him
Tania's pillow.' [*Her voice cracks.*] If you
don't want me any more you could at least
have the guts to tell me.

PETER: Of course I want you.

SUZANNE: It's pretty obvious you want something else.

PETER: I'm very happy with you.

SUZANNE: If you were really happy with me I don't
think you'd want to be looking at a load of
Danish prostitutes with their legs apart.

PETER: They're just bodies.

SUZANNE: That's the impression I got.

PETER: It's just something I needed now and then.

SUZANNE: Like going to the lavatory.

PETER: Every so often I need to *look* at a woman's body.

SUZANNE: But not mine.

PETER: Of course I want to look at you. I very much want to look at you.

SUZANNE: Like *that?*
[*He turns.*]

PETER: Yes!
[*A pause.*]

SUZANNE: When I found those pictures today I felt — degraded.

PETER: I'm sorry.

SUZANNE: Well, don't ask me to be *like* them!

PETER: I don't.

SUZANNE: I don't want to be looked at like that.

PETER: I know.

SUZANNE: I want to be made *love* to.

PETER: Cuddly.

SUZANNE: What does that mean?

PETER: You like to be cuddled ... You like to be cuddled and touched ... in the dark. On your back. Always in bed ... You like to be warm and wrapped up and ... cuddled.

SUZANNE: What you're saying is I'm boring.

PETER: I enjoy it.

SUZANNE: You don't have to patronise me.

PETER: I do enjoy it!

SUZANNE: Wouldn't you rather I went down to the station in my nightie and had my picture taken in that automatic thing?

PETER: How can I explain if you're just going to be nasty?

SUZANNE: I don't think I'm the nasty one in the family.

PETER: If you think I'm that revolting do you want me to leave?

SUZANNE: I don't know.

PETER: I see.

SUZANNE: I'm still thinking about it. What about the rest of the pictures?

PETER: What about them?

SUZANNE: Aren't you going to take them down?

PETER: I'll take them down later.

SUZANNE: What are you going to do with them?

PETER: Throw them away . . . That's what you want, isn't it?

SUZANNE: Not if you're only doing it because I found them . . . Can you do without them?

PETER: I don't know.

SUZANNE: Do you think you're ill?

PETER: No.

SUZANNE: Are you perverted?

PETER: No.

SUZANNE: So it's something you *choose* to do?

PETER: It helps . . . that's all.

SUZANNE: You don't see anything unpleasant about it?

PETER: It's like the Instant Milk you keep in the cupboard in case we run out. It's not as good as the real thing but it's better than nothing.

SUZANNE: I'm nothing.

PETER: It's better than lying in bed at night with you, wanting you, not getting off to sleep with you right next to me doing a good impersonation of an anaesthetist's practice dummy . . . I mean, if I don't make a quick jump in the three seconds between you putting the light out and falling asleep, I've had it. I ought to be in the Olympics . . . How do you do it . . . ? Seriously? Do you slip yourself a quick Mickey Finn with the drinking chocolate?

SUZANNE: I can't help being a good sleeper.

PETER: You make Rip Van Winkle look like an insomniac.

SUZANNE: Maybe you could give me a few clues beforehand, so I know what to expect ... You spend the entire evening dividing your attention between the television and the *Financial Times* and then when I'm nice and warm and sleepy you leap on me with all the delicacy of a high diver and expect me to behave like the Irma la Douce of Darwin Close ... You're a fine one to talk about Instant Milk.

PETER: I've given up trying.

SUZANNE: I'm glad you agree.

PETER: For the last ten years any attempt on my part to seduce you has been met with the erotic cry 'Wait Until Bedtime ...' and when bedtime comes, we know what happens, don't we?

SUZANNE: When have you ever tried to seduce me? Your idea of a passionate advance is holding hands during *The Money Programme*.

PETER: Hold hands ...? You must be joking. You'd have to put your knitting down.

SUZANNE: You want to be thankful I make most of my own things. You'd soon notice the difference if I went and bought them ... D'you know how much that dress I made today cost? 20p!

PETER: If you spent as much time taking your clothes off as you do putting them on, none of this would have happened.

SUZANNE: So it's all my fault.

PETER: It's nobody's fault ... We're just different, that's all.

SUZANNE: I don't see why I should do things I don't like to satisfy your peculiar fantasies.

PETER: I don't see why I should do without them because you don't want them. I'm getting sick of being a human Teddy bear.

SUZANNE: Don't be so pathetic.

PETER: Don't you have any fantasies?

SUZANNE: Not like yours.

PETER: A row of shiny dishwashers grappling with a new food mixer?

SUZANNE: You would think the only fantasy I'm likely to have involves a set of kitchen utensils!

PETER: So what do you think about in that minute fraction of a second before you go to sleep?

SUZANNE: Nothing.

PETER: I believe you.

SUZANNE: That doesn't mean I don't think about things when I'm washing the dishes or peeling the potatoes.

PETER: Go on then ... What excites you ...? I mean, I've never really found out ... What is it ...? Skinheads ...? A whole truckload of Samurai warriors ...? Michael Parkinson?

SUZANNE: I think about you.

PETER: What do I do to you? Force you to take sleeping pills?

SUZANNE: I think about you in the bank. I think, well at least he's getting somewhere. I may be bored out of my mind, but it's helping Peter.

PETER: I don't want to be helped.

SUZANNE: You expect the house to be nice.

PETER: I want you to be happy.

SUZANNE: You've made that very clear.

PETER: That's why I married you.

SUZANNE: 'With all my worldly goods I thee endow ...' and make sure you keep them polished!

PETER: I think there's a bit more to it than that.

SUZANNE: Oh ... would you like a few words on Love, Honour and Cherish?

PETER: Try 'With my body I thee worship!'

[*A long pause. The mood goes down to a quieter level.*]

SUZANNE: I thought we were all right ... Safe, I suppose ... You've always been kind and thoughtful ... I thought the only thing missing was children, and I've got used to that ... I've seen other people break up and I've thought, we're all right.

PETER: I don't enjoy it, you know ... Not really ... Many's the time I've rushed home with a new book and then in ten minutes I've seen it all and ... it's all over. There's nobody there.

SUZANNE: Not so much as a goosepimple.

PETER: Maggie's day on the beach ... There's a lot of goosepimples in that ... too many.

SUZANNE: Why do they do it?

PETER: Money.

SUZANNE: How could anybody do that for money?

PETER: I suppose if they didn't enjoy it they could always get a job in the bank.

SUZANNE: D'you know, I've never seen people ... like that before.

PETER: And it makes you feel sick.

SUZANNE: Not any more ... it's ... well ... a bit ridiculous ... It hasn't got anything to do with the way I feel ... When did you look at them?

PETER: Sunday morning mostly.

[*There is a slight revival of* SUZANNE'*s shocked voice.*]

SUZANNE: When I'm in church?

PETER: You've got your needs and I've got mine.

SUZANNE: It's not the same thing at all.

PETER: Of course it's not ... unless that Vicar's a bit more with it than I thought.

SUZANNE: That Vicar, as you call him, is doing his best to get all that banned.

[PETER *now begins to get angry.*]

PETER: What's he got to offer instead?

SUZANNE: Don't be ridiculous.

PETER: Well, come on ... What's he got to offer me ... ? The only useful thing he's ever done is marry us. I mean, he told us to love one another but he wasn't exactly forthcoming with the technical know-how, was he?

SUZANNE: Well I think he's right.

PETER: If I was as keen on banning things I don't have any use for, he'd be out of a job for a start.

SUZANNE: Well, if it wasn't there you wouldn't want it.

PETER: If it wasn't there maybe I'd want the real thing.

SUZANNE: You do anyway.

PETER: I manage without.

SUZANNE: You'd love to go to bed with Val, to name but one, but you haven't got the guts to do it, that's all.

PETER: I wish you hadn't said that.

SUZANNE: Yes, well, the truth does hurt.

PETER: When are you going to understand it's because I love you ... ? Even if you are a bit stuffy ... even if you do prefer a good knit to a good ... screw ... ! I chose second best ... I chose hiding in corners ... I chose a two-dimensional substitute for what I really need because I love you ... I don't want another woman! I don't want to live anywhere else with anybody else ... I don't want to share my sex life with a load of paper and ink ... I don't want Wendy's everlasting bath or Stephanie's forty-nine inch bust, or stupid stories about girls who forgot to wear their knickers to the office ...

[*He stops and turns away.*]

SUZANNE: They're feeding on you! They're making a fortune! You can't buy love over a counter.

PETER: So that's your message to all the lonely little men up and down the country, is it ... ? Ban porn and put computer dating on the National Health.

SUZANNE: One minute you say you don't want it and the next you're up on your soapbox telling me to leave it alone.

PETER: Before you clear the slums you've got to build some new houses.

SUZANNE: There has got to be something better.

PETER: Of course there's something better. And I and several million others aren't getting it ... It's all right for you. You get what you want.

SUZANNE: Rubbish.

PETER: All right, so you're frustrated.

SUZANNE: Spending all day in this place is enough to turn anybody into a zombie.

PETER: D'you think I enjoy going to the bank?

SUZANNE: Of course you do.

PETER: I don't have any choice.

SUZANNE: You do meet people. You do have somebody to talk to.

PETER: There's nothing to stop you talking to anybody.

SUZANNE: Who is there to talk to round here?

PETER: There's lots of people.

SUZANNE: Oh yes ... The butcher, the baker, the candlestick maker!

PETER: Well, get a job then.

SUZANNE: I haven't got any qualifications.

PETER: You've got your G.C.E.

SUZANNE: What's that worth now?

PETER: Well, get some more. Sign up for the Open University. Do a teaching course.

SUZANNE: I wouldn't have enough time for the housework.

PETER: I'll help you.
[*Pause.*]

SUZANNE: Are you trying to buy me?

PETER: I'm trying to give you something.
[*Pause.*]

SUZANNE: I'll think about it.

PETER: Go on. Be a student. You'd look nice in jeans.

[SUZANNE *gets up and turns on the TV. Up comes the title sequence of* The Money Programme. *Then* PETER *gets up and turns it off.*]

SUZANNE: You don't have to turn it off.

PETER: I don't want to watch it ... Let's go out somewhere.

SUZANNE: There's nothing on at the pictures.

PETER: Let's go out and have a meal.

SUZANNE: You are trying to buy me.

PETER: I bought you a long time ago. Now I just want to convince you.

SUZANNE: Is it going to stop?

PETER: Yes.

SUZANNE: And no more?

PETER: Eventually.

SUZANNE: I see.

PETER: It's difficult.

SUZANNE: I don't see why.

PETER: I've got a subscription.

SUZANNE: Can't you stop it?

PETER: It was a cheap deal.

SUZANNE: Does that mean they've got more clothes or less?

[PETER *pulls a face at her. Pause.*]

Well ... I suppose we'll both have to make an effort.

[PETER *nods wearily. She holds her hand out. He comes to her and they kiss, perhaps slightly as though they'd never done it before.*]

Did you say we were going out for a meal?

PETER: What do you fancy?

SUZANNE: Curry.

PETER: Curries have strong aphrodisiac properties.

SUZANNE: Are you frightened?

PETER: Just thought I'd mention it.

SUZANNE: They just make me sweat.

PETER: I like you when you sweat.

SUZANNE: Is that why you won't buy me a floor polisher?

PETER: Let's go.

SUZANNE: I want to put my new dress on.

PETER: You do that.

> [*She goes out. After a moment he follows. He stands looking at the photographs on the left wall, then goes along taking them down and screwing them up. He arrives at the bedroom door. He walks into the bedroom.*]

What are we going to do about Val?

> [SUZANNE *is taking her dress off — and underslip. She attempts the same kind of defiant sexuality that we'd seen earlier.* PETER *walks behind her and is reflected in the mirror.*]

SUZANNE: Val's not coming. I was lying.

> [PETER *is touched by her attempts and is beginning to be turned on. They kiss and move to the bed. They lie down. He touches her.*]
> [*Fade.*]

THE END

Rosemary Mason

SUNBEAMS

Sunbeams was first produced at the Soho Poly, London, on 26th April, 1976. It was directed by John Link and designed by Harry Duffin, with the following cast:

LOUISE	Sandy Ratcliff
MAN	Andrew Hislop
FRANCES	Bridget Brice

Characters

LOUISE, a prostitute
FRANCES, a social worker
MAN

SCENE ONE
A room in noisy darkness.
We see only the outline of a closed door lit from the outside, and feel the strobing of a colour television angled away from us into the room. The volume is turned down. The moving outline of a couple merges into the mass of a large bed, the whole almost indistinguishable from the shadow of the room.

MAN: Bitch!

> [*This is accompanied by a healthy slap. After a second's pause a woman moans at length.*]

More?

WOMAN: No, no. Please — no more!

> [*A second slap is followed equally unspontaneously by a gusty yell. We are aware of the sound of running feet descending the stair from the floor above. The man administers a third slap and again comes the requisite scream, this time accompanied by an urgent banging on the door.*]

FRANCES: Please — please, are you all right?

> [*The scream dribbles out.*]

For God's sake stop hitting her!

> [*And the curses of the two accompany the frenzied activity of dressing in the dark.*]

Hang on, I'll get the police.

> [*Feet are heard to run away down the corridor.*]

MAN: Sod off!

WOMAN: It's that cow downstairs.

> [*The feet return.*]

FRANCES: Please! [*banging with new energy*] Speak to me please!

MAN: [*dashing for the door*] It's a bleedin' raid!
[*He opens the door. The flood of light momentarily encapsulates the whole scene — like some candid camera.*]
[*Outside is* FRANCES, *in her early twenties, neat but flustered, apprehensive and yet wholeheartedly concerned. The* MAN, *small, in mangy middle age, his face the colour of bloater paste, his hand anchoring his flies, pauses momentarily.*]
Oh shit!
[*He disappears, braces flying.*]
[*Inside,* LOUISE, *legs astride, stands facing the door, her neat bottom towards us. She is wearing thigh boots and G-string and a distinctly incongruous T-shirt. She is slapping her boot with the stick of a multicoloured feather duster — it has the same significance as the wagging of a cat's tail.*]

LOUISE: Well, hello Sunshine!
[*The edge of the greeting increases* FRANCES' *confusion at the lady's get-up. She is still outside the door.*]

FRANCES: Oh, I think I ... well, I thought ...!

LOUISE: Are they coming?

FRANCES: Who?

LOUISE: The fuzz.

FRANCES: Oh no — er, I never actually called them — well, he's gone, hasn't he?

LOUISE: Without paying.

FRANCES: Paying! [*and the dawn of truth*] Oh Christ!
[LOUISE *turns away from the door. We see her face for the first time — she is virtually unmade-up, fresh-faced*

> *and healthy and while the lower part of her body conforms to the custom of her trade, the upper part could be that of a student. In an attempt to explain her mistake,* FRANCES *comes into the room.*]

Oh — I only thought you were being hurt, or murdered even . . . that something awful was happening to you . . . so I thought . . . I thought I'd better . . .

> [*Silence.* LOUISE *ambles towards the bed. She picks up the paper, slumps and reads.*]

I'm Frances Partington from upstairs.

> [LOUISE *looks up, gazing directly, unmoved.*]

Well, we have to be so careful . . . don't we . . . that is, careful of each other . . . for each other . . . no community any more, just awful isolation . . .

> [*Stunned silence from* LOUISE.]

If we could only care for, well, love each other . . . properly . . . everyone included . . . that's what's wrong in a city like this, each of us a . . . a separate maggot in his very own apple . . . silently munching his soul.

> [LOUISE, *bored with it all, pulls the paper over her face.*]

LOUISE: Piss off — maggot!

> [FRANCES, *slain, hesitates only momentarily before turning to leave.*]

Don't go, silly bitch!

> [LOUISE *leaps from the bed and whoops maniacally towards the door.* FRANCES *turns, startled but freezing.*]

FRANCES: Oh, I quite distinctly got the impression you wanted me to.

[LOUISE, *who has forgotten about her lost earnings by now, has warmed considerably, sensing a chase. She puts on the light, slams the door and rescues her jeans from the floor. The room is a toyshop of the equipment of the oldest profession. A large mirror is angled over the bed. A large Teddy bear remains uncorrupted. The bed is the centre of the room.*]

LOUISE: [*hopping about, getting into her jeans*] No need to get ratty, Frances. You'll soon get used to me.

[*She rushes* FRANCES *to the bed and pushes her to sit.* FRANCES, *reluctant to sit on a bed of such recent memories, sits anxiously.* LOUISE *scoops up the feather duster, laughing.*]

Me and my little ways. [*She slings the duster into space.*] With your training it's a cinch.

FRANCES: Training?

LOUISE: The old cow downstairs says you're a social worker.

FRANCES: [*thawing and distinctly pleased at the interest*] Yes, I am — it took time, to qualify of course, getting a degree — but yes, I am . . . with the Council. It's quite a good position.

[LOUISE *laughs.*]

A very good position.

LOUISE: Are you good?

FRANCES: Well, I think so.

LOUISE: You just seem a bit too . . .

FRANCES: Too what?

LOUISE: New, I suppose.

FRANCES: Well, I'm newly qualified but that doesn't mean I'm not good.

LOUISE: No, I suppose not, but . . .

FRANCES: Oh no, I've worked very hard for this . . .

LOUISE: I could mean wet, really.
[*The echo of schooldays requires action.* FRANCES *picks up a black negligee draped on the bed.*]

FRANCES: No, we just have different standards ... [*folding the garment*] ... different priorities.
[*She changes her mind and lets the negligee fall in a heap.*]

LOUISE: Not exactly wet wet, more inexperienced — a virgin perhaps?

FRANCES: I am *not* a virgin.

LOUISE: Technically no, but you always will be, won't you? [*breezily grabbing up the negligee*] Within every whore, within every woman, lurks a virgin screaming to get out ... [*She chucks the negligee lazily on the floor.*] ... silently mouthing, bound and gagged even, but screaming all the same.
[*Professional custom can only allow* FRANCES *to dismiss such speculation.*]

FRANCES: No, no, no, that's hardly likely, is it?

LOUISE: Oh ... you're speaking from experience are you?

FRANCES: No — but people wouldn't, women wouldn't do it all the time if they didn't enjoy it!

LOUISE: Not just to get what they really want — companionship, a family, safety? No, it's deeper — I mean that bleak middle of it all feeling — when a man is pounding away inside you like you're some unopened door.

FRANCES: Knock and the door will be opened!

LOUISE: Not this one. Your virgin self is shoving with all its might on the other side — and anyway, often it's locked and you threw away the key. [*mock dramatics*] You scream in the deep night, but rescue can only come ...

FRANCES: Through the door ... very dramatic but

hardly relevant.

LOUISE: But you don't know the *feeling* do you? Yet you speculate about some maggoty isolation — 'modern living' or is that all theory, part of the job, sociology?

FRANCES: And are you telling me you peddle true love?

LOUISE: Truer than yours.

FRANCES: But *I* don't do it for the money!

LOUISE: But I need more than you, for being a bad girl. What's your rent?

FRANCES: Thirty-two pounds per calendar month, plus heating.

LOUISE: Ah well, my flat's so hot it costs treble that.

FRANCES: That's nearly a hundred pounds — oh heaven, you've got to appeal ... you've a strong case — you *must* ... Landlords! God I hate them. I'll help you with the forms, I'd like to ... if you like?

> [*Unable to take* FRANCES' *ardour,* LOUISE *paces about.*]

LOUISE: I can read, you know. [*Spotting a new toy, she laughs.*] I'm a professional lady.

> [*She plonks a mortarboard on her head.* FRANCES *coughs at the implication of the game and just manages a giggle.* LOUISE *has found the cane.*]

Asad Singh won't chuck me out, the *Abbey National* relies on my immoral earnings. [*The cane assumes the role of pointer.*] Can a landlord be sued for living off tainted money, Frances? Or the *Abbey* for that matter ... Maybe you could get a form. Can I appeal? Kick up a stink — what rotters people are — absolutely dreadful, Frances. And I pay my stamp, too. Can you stop *me* paying too much rent? No way, Frances, prosecute *him* for keeping a bawdy house — and I'm homeless.

> [*She slings the cane and hat into the corner.*]

[*cruel and low*] Maybe I could share with you, Frances.

> [FRANCES *shudders. But* LOUISE *has her hands on* FRANCES' *shoulders, face to face, uncomfortably near.*]

Whatever your mother says, you can't catch easy virtue from the lavatory seat, dear, it doesn't shoot up from the bowl and re-educate your 'hidden treasure'. If I touch you, breathe on you, kiss you . . . [*But* FRANCES *breaks free*] . . . you won't get nymphomania.

> [*The phone by the door starts ringing.*]

Because I haven't got it, you see. I'm a professional lady. I do a job. That's all.

> [*Pause. Eventually* LOUISE *crosses to the phone, picks it up and places her hand over the receiver. The caller burbles incoherently.* FRANCES *gets up and starts to move towards the door.*]

FRANCES: I must go . . . early start . . .

> [*But* LOUISE *moves across the doorway.*]

LOUISE: Can't we talk some more? Shall we? You can tell me your professional secrets and I'll tell you mine! [*laughing*] Compare notes. [*waving the phone*] Case to case. [*into the phone*] Hello — mm. Pardon? Who is this please?

> [FRANCES *paces about, unwilling to touch* LOUISE *to move her. During the telephone conversation* FRANCES *stoops to pick up the black negligee. She feels its alien slither — quite distinct from M & S. When* LOUISE

> *has perhaps turned away, she sneaks
> a pleasurably disgusted glimpse at
> herself in the overhead mirror,
> holding the garment to her.* LOUISE,
> *on the other hand, is not unaware.*]

[*abstractedly*] Long, long socks pulled up to
my ... [*The caller mumbles.*] Yesss, well
above my knees. [*The caller mumbles
approvingly.*] Just who are you, anyway?
[*The caller interjects briefly.*] Urges? What
urges? [*The caller speaks at length.*] OK.
Pink, actually, with green ribbons ... [*The
caller interrupts briefly.*] All right, blue,
then. [*The caller asks a question.*] Yes, of
course I'm a virgin, and no ... mummy
needn't know ... daddy won't hit you ...
well, you could ask him ... no, I haven't got
one ... no, of course it could be a danger ...
[*The caller gets animated.*] Yes, I'm sure you
... Oh, for Christ's sake, Henry you've had
half an hour today already — don't you feel
any better?

> [*Swiftly* FRANCES *folds the negligee
> and places it on the bed.*]

I can't talk, someone's here — don't you feel
you could branch out on a real ... [*The
caller makes distraught objections.*] ... call
— yes, to a stranger? You're very ... er ...
dominating, you know. [*turning to* FRANCES
and grimacing] Extremely ... Do it and ring
me, eh?

> [*She replaces the receiver.* FRANCES *is
> appalled at* LOUISE *yet flushed at her
> own near discovery.*]

FRANCES: Really! I have to make calls but what sort of
service are you running?

LOUISE: It's nothing ...

FRANCES: So, you're just teasing poor old thing ...

LOUISE: Henry.

FRANCES: You're just that sort of woman aren't you, who'll drive a man to violent sexual . . . acts. Stirring things up. Using his male vulnerability to build up dangerous pressure . . .

LOUISE: A time bomb primed to burst out on some Mrs Smith or other as she crosses the common after keep-fit classes!

FRANCES: Yes, he'll rape someone.

LOUISE: Well, she'll be able to run fast, won't she. 'Rabid Results College' — six-week graduate course in sexual deviation — only serious sex offenders need apply . . . Come off it — Henry's safely locked up in his own mind, a virgin child who somehow got chipped along with the nursery furniture . . .

FRANCES: Home psychology book three?

LOUISE: I can't help that can I? When he phones I'm supposed to pretend I don't know who he is. So today I broke the rules. All I know is *he* sends me a weekly postal order, crossed, and *I* receive his obscene calls.

FRANCES: Euh!

LOUISE: Which can't be bad, can it . . .? And I can read at the same time.

FRANCES: And watch telly . . .?

LOUISE: If I could read on the job I would — my mind's hardly occupied, dear — as it is, it's often better to occupy my eyes elsewhere . . .

FRANCES: Heaven, you really hate men, don't you . . . You'd like to see them deprived of all their pride and energy . . .

LOUISE: Huh . . . Me Tarzan.
[*She blows a diminishing raspberry.*]

FRANCES: [*bravely ignoring the sentiment*] . . . with sex reduced to a function that pays well — I expect you cheat your clients, don't you?

LOUISE: If that's what the book says!

FRANCES: You don't care for them, even as other human beings . . . nothing. Some needy,

needing man climbs your stair for comfort
...

LOUISE: Poor little man ...

FRANCES: ... he's a human, a human ...

LOUISE: Cashcard?

FRANCES: ... a human being and you don't even pretend to care.

LOUISE: Pretending's not part of the deal any more. Anyway, who pretends they care for me — am I so disgusting?

FRANCES: Yes!

LOUISE: Is my honesty any worse than the pretended excitement that coos its way around suburban front bedrooms on a Saturday night? Men acting tough — when inside they're weedy and little — scared to be themselves. Who ever responds with honesty? At least when women laid back and thought of England many *honestly* hated 'that sort of thing' ... Now a quick read of *Nova*, and a late night movie and we've all got the routine patter of oohs and ahs to be *dishonestly* liberated — overjoyed at sex. But how many women still plan the next day's menu while hubby works his way up to an undignified coronary? God no! I can't pretend any more, not just to be kind.

FRANCES: If you hate sex and people I'd say you're definitely in the wrong job!

LOUISE: Look, Sunshine, if you can come up with a Careers Guidance Officer who can place someone like me — stuck in a large bed, shit-scared by a twenty-two by fifteen inch glimpse of 'out there', and too scared to join in, invite them to tea!

FRANCES: [*smoothing her skirt*] Really?

[LOUISE *gazes up at the dwarfed image of herself in the mirror,*

> *pushing up her breasts with her hands, then letting them go.*]

LOUISE: How can I be the prostitute with the heart of gold when I want to join in the real game . . .? If I stay here with all the freaks, how will I ever find out if there is . . . anything?

> [FRANCES *gets up from the bed, crosses to the television and contemplates its message flatly.*]

FRANCES: Perhaps there isn't a 'real game' — and they're all as freaky as . . . me.

> [LOUISE *goes to her and gives her a cuddle cum rugby tackle.* FRANCES *stiffens.*]

LOUISE: Don't worry, duckie — half time. [*starting a slow waltz by herself*] I'm not queer nor do I hate men, two three, or people, or sex. [*with a final flurry*] I just hate me — and Jesus does not want me for a sunbeam.

> [*And she stands in quietness — unblessed. Now it is* FRANCES' *turn to put her arm around* LOUISE, *awkwardly, seriously.*]

FRANCES: Look, you don't have to be ashamed — ashamed of what you are, or do, or anything — I understand — somehow you've been led astray, somewhere in your background — influenced — and have taken a wrong turning, that's all. [LOUISE *breaks away.*] No one need know what you've been doing, need they? We'll keep it a secret . . .

LOUISE: I am not a sixties unmarried mum, thank you! I haven't anything to hide. And it's an insult to say I was merely led. No, I chose a career but now I've exhausted it, that's all.

FRANCES: Or it's exhausted you?

> [LOUISE *is wandering about frustratedly touching things. She picks*]

up a cat-o'-nine-tails and tugs at its thongs.]

LOUISE: That's just it — it hasn't, has it? I'm bored as hell, like some flabby executive whose promotion's frozen 'cos his boss won't die . . . I don't eagerly satisfy the merest whim of my clients any more, proud to serve. Noted for my adaptability. Where's the future in being tied to the bed — scared they'll leave you to starve! Brilliant career prospects offered young ladies willing to lay down their lives . . .

FRANCES: It's not a career!

LOUISE: It is, you know . . . I used to be able to lay down for all occasions — long, short, fancy, functional — but now it's just a job and a job I've outgrown.

FRANCES: [*bitterly*] So what's the next step, an establishment of your own!

LOUISE: I'm not guilty of anything, Frances. They reckon we have to change our careers at least four times and retrain for something new. That's the stage I'm at. So I've weedy clients — less energy's needed from me.

[*The phone rings.* LOUISE *crosses to it.*]

Some never quite manage it. [*with her hand over the mouthpiece*] But I don't despise them for it. [*into the phone*] Hello. [*covering the mouthpiece*] Then there's Henry . . . [*waving the phone*] who I've never met, anyway. [*There is a mounting burble from the caller.* LOUISE *replies in mock reaction.*] Really.

FRANCES: What do you get — just the horrid money?

LOUISE: [*into the phone*] How disgusting! Young man, I shall have to tell the operator. [*covering the mouthpiece*] There's the fringe benefits — I lipread extremely fluently . . .

[*into the phone*] Piss off for Christ's sake!
[*Exclamations from the caller.*]

> [LOUISE *explains to* FRANCES, *who has grown quite concerned for Henry.*]

I just can't ... not today.

> [FRANCES *capably takes the phone.*]

FRANCES: Hello, who is this? [*The caller burbles obscenely.*] You're a very sick boy ... and my knickers are no concern of yours. [*The caller blows a raspberry.*] You need help, you're ... [*The caller hangs up.*] ... sick.

LOUISE: [*with bitter applause*] So much for field work.

FRANCES: But you can't just give him what he wants all the time, that's not what he *needs*.

LOUISE: Not what *you* think he needs, no. But carbolic doesn't help his erection.

FRANCES: That's just *it*!

LOUISE: He shouldn't have one?

FRANCES: No! Well, not like that.

LOUISE: What you going to do — put salt on his tail?

FRANCES: Of course not!

LOUISE: And if he can't get one any other way?

FRANCES: There's therapy and understanding and ...

LOUISE: And if understanding doesn't turn him on?

FRANCES: No — not so physically, but it would help.

LOUISE: Help him not to go blind, or mad — you could tie his hands to his cot.

FRANCES: You know they don't think like that any more.

LOUISE: No, but you do. He gets great pleasure from his own body — *I* give him the incentive, *I* excite him — *I* relieve the pressure ... [*mockingly*] ... the pressure that kills!

FRANCES: But you're not God. He is a potential danger to society — you just postpone it, that's all — you don't stop it.

LOUISE: So your sociology lark is a new form of

lobotomy, is it? It'll neutralise Henry, will it?

FRANCES: Well, of course we don't claim to cure everything — not at all — but by understanding the causes ...

LOUISE: You will be in full possession of the facts ...

FRANCES: Yes and we'd get the right treatment for him.

LOUISE: And then?

FRANCES: Well, after a psychiatrist ...

LOUISE: You'll make him unhappy by trying to fit him into your pattern of what's normal. He's a discreet but apathetic wanker — that bothers you?

FRANCES: Yes!

LOUISE: And yet it doesn't seem to bother Henry.

FRANCES: But ...

LOUISE: While you're busy changing Henry from one kind of freak to another, babies are dying hungry. Old people die and rot and almost disappear before *you* — understanding bloody lot — can notice they've stopped breathing. I know my lot are breathing, I can smell it!

FRANCES: Yes, there are inevitably problems ... huge errors of —

LOUISE: Christ!

FRANCES: But we can't just pick out the cases willy-nilly according to an emotional points system.

LOUISE: Why not?

FRANCES: Our net must be uniformly wide to catch *everyone* who needs us.

LOUISE: You think in bloody thousands.

FRANCES: For efficiency's sake.

LOUISE: But not for theirs?

FRANCES: Yes ... I mean, no, no ...

LOUISE: Wanker! Getting cheap thrills out of understanding the poor sods, wholesale.

FRANCES: No, no, what I'm saying is that I must . . . try to care deeply for *all* of them regardless of . . . natural preferences, within a . . .

LOUISE: [*laughing, unconvinced*] Yes . . . [*getting up and striding to a shelf and squirting perfume down her front and gazing at herself in a small mirror*] Like it doesn't bother you in the least that I'm a prostitute. [*pulling at her eyelid*] Failed. You cough politely when they fart and ignore their emotional needs.

> [*Pause.* FRANCES *shuffles and smooths herself — a last appeal to civilised understanding.*]

FRANCES: It's a pretty bloody job, you know.

LOUISE: It would be . . . [FRANCES *is slightly relieved.*] . . . to you. [*shouting*] Grow up, girly! Peter Pan was queer.

> [FRANCES *stands up and snatches up a schoolgirl's boater. She punches it.*]

FRANCES: Typical! Reduce everything to a . . . [*restoring the hat at* LOUISE's *look*] . . . sick joke!

LOUISE: You're the only bloody joke around here.

FRANCES: [*her hackles risen*] Me? [*She slowly twirls the hat on her finger — an accusation. It is her turn to take her time.*] So why hasn't our oldest profession succeeded where my newer one . . . ?

LOUISE: [*swift and low, stalking*] Because it deals in basic physical necessity . . . [*snatching the hat*] . . . like yours deals in material needs not gut feelings. I admit it's an alternative not better or worse than what you call normal . . . [*skimming the hat across the bed*] . . . just different. *I* never set it up as a cure-all — it's a job but it's closer to what's important. You've gone and cut out even that. Play an hour in someone's fantasy and you don't

have to open your eyes *very* wide to see a man
in his socks, at his most vulnerable. If you
must be a bloody Messiah — that's the time
to do it surely!

FRANCES: ... I ... I don't profess to be a Saviour but
I've always known there must be a right
direction to be going ...

LOUISE: You had a vision in the school bog!

FRANCES: No. But I suppose I do come from a
Christian family.

LOUISE: A deprived childhood ...

FRANCES: My mother taught me to *expect* to serve.

LOUISE: But to hang on to your knickers ...

FRANCES: We knew how lucky we were and must ...

LOUISE: Salve your consciences.

FRANCES: No, not that, but must disperse our material
and spiritual plenty to those who had less.

> [LOUISE *holds up her fingers in the
> blessing but it reverts to a V-sign —
> spitting out her truth.*]

LOUISE: [*shouting*] It's bloody pity! [*grabbing at*
FRANCES' *chin*] Horrible treacly muck!

> [FRANCES *pushes her off more
> violently than she'd meant to.*]

FRANCES: No! No! it's *not*!

> [*But* LOUISE *slaps* FRANCES' *face.*]

LOUISE: Po-faced bitch!

FRANCES: [*more shocked than hurt*] How can I discuss
anything?

LOUISE: With me? Can't, I'm a dirty pervert.

FRANCES: *I* never said that.

LOUISE: But you've thought it.

FRANCES: [*by now tears are welling*] No — no I have
not. [*But her look about the room denies
this.*] How can I have had *your* experiences
when I'm *me*?

LOUISE: Yes, well, that's what I object to.

> [FRANCES *eyes* LOUISE *suspiciously
> as* LOUISE *circles the room, picking*

up, handling and kicking her things. She picks up a pair of startling briefs and flexes the elastic. When FRANCES *is sure that* LOUISE *is farthest from the door she moves swiftly towards it and opens it. But* LOUISE *darts violently to the open door and pulls* FRANCES *squealing back into the room, slamming the door shut.*]

You were born squealing ... [*pushing her around the room*] ... screaming in disgust just like your mother was appalled at ever having fucked — Yes, it *is* crude!

FRANCES: Please! Please! Don't be so ... There's no need!

LOUISE: And it's rude.

[LOUISE *lets* FRANCES *go then dances about maniacally, waving the briefs about* FRANCES' *face.* FRANCES *bats off the offensive garment.*]

[*laughing*] Crikey, isn't it rude, Frances! But we all come from the same place.

[*She makes a grab at* FRANCES' *crutch.* FRANCES *doubles and cries out, sinking to her knees moaning, but* LOUISE *holds up her face to the light.*]

When did you ever let anyone in there for love? Don't you just pity men?

FRANCES: I've had lovers ...

[LOUISE'S *grip is softer, gentler. She smooths back* FRANCES' *hair.*]

LOUISE: The men who insinuate, tell their troubles — and pop before you know it's in. Were they men?

FRANCES: But I ...

LOUISE: Objects — of your pity.

[LOUISE *lets go and walks to look up into the mirror.*]

FRANCES: [*still kneeling*] I loved some ... one ... [*picking up the briefs beside her, stroking the satin*] But he couldn't stay.

LOUISE: Smothered.

FRANCES: He went.

LOUISE: [*lighter, swinging round from the mirror*] You're stuck with it, lovey — but for God's sake learn how to use it!

FRANCES: I would like to love.

LOUISE: [*laughing low*] Love? That's a word.

FRANCES: [*settling back on her heels*] My parents ... always ask whether I've found ... my calling. And I try to believe. But the idea never develops into a ... real feeling. Like help, I suppose, never grows into love — just pity.

LOUISE: [*musing, picking up Teddy and stroking his ear*] Mmmmm. Love?

FRANCES: I see it as concern, I suppose. But I don't know how to make it — gracious.

LOUISE: [*at last, lightly*] And I see it as — a cuddle.
        [*And Teddy receives a cuddle gratefully.*]

FRANCES: But I thought ...

LOUISE: Not this lot — I must mean a concerned cuddle. [*to Teddy*] Not had one lately. [*grinning*] Though I could have missed it. [*And Teddy takes flight.*]

FRANCES: When you get so close to people?

LOUISE: I'm miles and miles away.

FRANCES: You *could* ... help them.

LOUISE: No, gracious lady ... [*giving her a pat on the head*] ... but *you* could. I've worked at it too long ... [*a pause and a smile*] It's taken the whole of my youth, my childhood even. When you're ugly and spotty and quiet, well, you desperately need to be *good* at something, don't you? So, at thirteen, if you're the only girl who'll take her knickers off, you develop, well, a certain following. I became prettier as I grew up but the habit stuck. I became sexually adept. A sex machine. Very, very capable. People don't need to know a machine and machines tend not to get hurt. So, like some endless production, lovers were processed and the machine's too busy in the performance to receive anything ... And a machine, is a machine, is a machine ...

[*And the television strobes on.*]

[*eventually*] So! What shall we do with our self-knowledge, hey? Change the course of it all. What do you want, Fran?

FRANCES: Well ... just to help, them ... people, you know — help, sort it out. And you?

LOUISE: Oh, to be *very, very* good at something.

SCENE TWO

Another day. Same room.

The bed has undergone a transformation: it is cleanly and neatly made. The assorted debris — wellingtons, the Teddy bear, and all the paraphernalia of LOUISE's *career — are regimented in meticulous order along the floor.*

FRANCES *is fully dressed, hair smoothed. She is seated neatly on the end of the bed, reading the paper. The television is off.* LOUISE *enters in her coat, loaded down with books.*

LOUISE: How did it go?

FRANCES: Oh, he's gone.

LOUISE: Which one?

FRANCES: That Cedric.

[LOUISE *shrugs, not knowing.*]

Tuesdays at three.

LOUISE: Mmmm.

FRANCES: Only he isn't.

LOUISE: Isn't what?

FRANCES: Called Cedric, it's a pseudonym, an alias.

LOUISE: As *I* never asked his name it seems rather superfluous, doesn't it?

FRANCES: Oh, it's not for anonymity — it's a punishment.

LOUISE: Kinky!

FRANCES: Lou!

LOUISE: Sorry.

FRANCES: His real name's Richard but he's so ashamed of himself, his inability to get on or prosper, that he's sort of confiscated his own name until he feels he deserves it back — don't you understand?

LOUISE: Well, I can understand that 'Cedric' is quite a punishment but the reasoning is so . . .

FRANCES: Sad?

LOUISE: Puritanical.

FRANCES: Well, he is — isn't he?

LOUISE: God knows. [*dumping the books on the bed*] He preferred the gloom and usually closed his eyes . . . still, that suits a beginner like you, doesn't it?

FRANCES: Well, he can't see me grit my teeth, no. But we only made it the first time — he just wants to chat and have a sort of cosy afternoon tea — he's coming twice next week.

LOUISE: I hope he's paying?

FRANCES: But that wouldn't be fair!

LOUISE: Be sensible. If you're not going to work for the Council any more you need the money.

FRANCES: Not from my old 'cases' though.

LOUISE: . . . No wonder you're drawing the crowds, dear, if you don't charge.

FRANCES: Just because they prefer the new management . . . Jealousy is a totally destructive emotion, Louise — you told me that. Think constructively, adapt to the new situation. Has it occurred to you that perhaps I give them something they need more?

LOUISE: Come off it! You've hardly graduated, have
you. It takes more than a dozen lousy
sessions — believe me. Don't underrate the
business — and it is a business, not a charity.

FRANCES: And where did your years of practice get you?
Anyway, talking's much harder, isn't it?

LOUISE: [*grandly*] Conversation always eluded *me* —
I just purred so they knew the current was
on. [*And she kicks the Teddy bear who is on
the floor.*] How the bloody hell should I
know!

> [*She finds a space on the bed and
> starts rapidly looking through her
> books.*]

FRANCES: And college?

> [LOUISE *puts one book down and
> picks up another.*]

LOUISE: Arguments. And the noise — twittering in
the space between my ears. If that's
'communication' I'm done for.

FRANCES: But you've only been there three half days.

LOUISE: So?

FRANCES: You dare let me down — super ruddy woman
— I've given up my job to keep you.

LOUISE: So! What does that make me? A pimp?

FRANCES: No, of course not . . . I just wanted to help
you.

LOUISE: Well, you're not allowed to 'just want to
help' *me*. That's too easy.

FRANCES: Easy! Do you think it all just happened . . .?
I've worked hard too, you know.

LOUISE: Liar! Go on, smother it in righteousness,
then you won't feel guilty, will you? I've
heard you, in here, laughing — laughing
with men . . . bloody enjoying it. Don't give
me that old martyr story . . . you couldn't
wait to get stuck in.

FRANCES: That's not true, not true at all.

LOUISE: I should have known when I first saw your

FRANCES: feeble little smile what you were after ... my
            job. Well, you've got it now but don't
            imagine you're going to use me as part of
            your holy orgasm ... find another sucker.

FRANCES: But you wanted to ... get out ... and ...

LOUISE: And don't think I can't see where it's leading
            ... I end up with nothing!

FRANCES: And the money? Mine.

LOUISE: And you'll get all the satisfaction.

FRANCES: The love?

            [*The phone rings.*]

            Come off it ...

            [LOUISE *goes angrily to the phone
            but* FRANCES *gets there first.*]

            9428. Yes. [*She covers the mouthpiece.*] But
            they can't give it, they're not capable.

            [*There is heavy breathing from the
            caller.*]

LOUISE: But you're going to screw it out of them,
            aren't you?

FRANCES: [*into the phone*] Who is this please? [*to
            LOUISE*] Screw it?

            [*Remembering the mouthpiece, she
            covers it — but Henry has heard. He
            responds with high-pitched
            appreciation.*]

LOUISE: Yes, gratitude — you've discovered the fuck
            and now you're trying to make everyone love
            you for it.

FRANCES: [*into the phone*] Now Henry, you know you
            don't want to know that.

            [*She covers the mouthpiece.*]

LOUISE: Including me!

FRANCES: [*into the phone*] Henry, that's rude!

LOUISE: [*dancing around, shouting*] But you like it
            rude — go on, meanie, tell him what colour
            your knickers are and sod the psychology.

FRANCES: [*calmly*] He needs understanding.

            [*She takes her hand down to speak.*]

LOUISE: [*loudly*] Understanding! He'd rather you smacked his bum.
[*The caller agrees lustily.*]

FRANCES: [*into the phone*] Look, Henry, you've got a problem, you must recognise that surely?
[*The caller grunts.*]

LOUISE: Hypocrite!

FRANCES: But you must let me ... help you.

LOUISE: [*shouting*] Don't believe it Henry, she's a raver ...

FRANCES: You can't *want* to be a phone freak all your life, surely?

LOUISE: [*heckling*] Hang onto your trousers Hen ...
[*The caller explains dejectedly.*]

FRANCES: Your hobby? But ... but it's a nasty dirty thing to do ... come on, Henry, isn't it? It's rude and naughty.
[*There is silence from the caller, followed by weeping.*]

LOUISE: [*to* FRANCES] Now look what you've done. [*She snatches the phone, picking up a yellow rubber mackintosh from the pile, and speaks as to a child.*] Hello big boy! I've, I've found this mackintosh — just here. [*The caller mumbles.*] It's yellow with a label that says 100% genuine rubber. [*The caller sighs.*] Shall I put it on? [*The caller assents.*]

FRANCES: Don't be stupid.

LOUISE: [*into the phone*] Mmmm, it's on. [*The caller responds enquiringly.*] Coooool and soft ... I can tuck my feet up. [*The caller gurgles.*] And my head in ... I can disappear.
[*The caller is by now drooling with appreciation.* LOUISE *is a yellow heap. She lets the receiver drop: the long silence is punctuated by mounting abuse from Henry.* FRANCES *crosses and replaces the receiver.* LOUISE, *snail-like, pokes her*

*head from her yellow shell, her face
tearstained.*]

Hold me please.

[FRANCES *responds, cuddling*
LOUISE, *gently stroking her hair.
There is room in the yellow
mackintosh for* FRANCES.]

FRANCES: [*low*] Time — lots of time. Bags we don't
practise on each other . . . and I'll stop trying
to make you grateful — honestly, and if you
ever need to . . . I understand it now . . . to *be*
with someone I can always take a day off and
you can . . .

LOUISE: [*breaking free and returning savagely to the
pile of books*] Don't worry piss-face — we'll
see who's good.

[*And she reads.* FRANCES *picks up the
mac, folds it neatly and returns it to
the pile.*]

[*We hear possibly the last chorus of*
Jesus wants me for a sunbeam.]

THE END

Also available from Amber Lane Press

Whose Life is it Anyway?   by Brian Clark

Can You Hear Me at the Back?   by Brian Clark

Once a Catholic   by Mary O'Malley

Look Out ... Here Comes Trouble!   by Mary O'Malley

Funny Peculiar   by Mike Stott

Piaf   by Pam Gems

*For information on these and forthcoming titles write
to:*
Amber Lane Press
Amber Lane Farmhouse
The Slack
ASHOVER
Derbyshire S45 0EB

WHOSE LIFE IS IT ANYWAY?

Brian Clark

Ken Harrison lies in a hospital bed, paralysed from the neck down following a car crash. He faces the prospect of being totally dependent on a life-support machine, realising that even the final option of suicide can be denied him. "If you're clever and sane enough to put up an invincible case for suicide," he says, "it demonstrates you ought not to die."

". . . a moving and absorbing drama about the struggle of a man for the right to die."

The Daily Telegraph

"Brian Clark has made a fascinating play out of this all too topical dilemma."

The Financial Times

PIAF

Pam Gems

Pam Gems writes . . .
In the world of popular music, there are two giants and they are both women — Billie Holiday and Edith Piaf. Piaf, the street-waif, rickety, illegitimate, became the supreme mistress of the chanson, influencing and launching almost a whole generation of French singers. What was it about this small, dumpy woman in the plain black dress, looking like a concierge? How did she do it? In the first place she was, despite illness and personal tragedy, a supreme technician. But she was also a woman who never became inflated, never forgot her roots, and who never became involved with materialism. For her, singing was ecstasy. She believed above all in love, physical love. When she sang, she sang as a woman, as an adult. She sang of sexuality and, when the mood was sad, of betrayal: you believed her. She had been there. The accuracy and reality of her work is unique in a world usually characterised by the banal and the commercial. Miraculously, in a sentimental genre, Piaf found emotional truth. This was her genius.

"Quite stunning. A genuinely warm portrait of a woman who found relief from the frequent unhappiness in her life in the orgasmic joy of singing."

The Guardian

"Everything about the Piaf legend comes across with potent force."

Daily Mail

QUEEN MARGARET COLLEGE LIBRARY